THE SCHOOL OF SPIRITUAL SCIENCE

An Introduction

Edited by Constanza Kaliks, Christiane Haid, Johannes Kühl, Claus-Peter Röh on behalf of the School's Leadership

TEMPLE LODGE

Temple Lodge Publishing Ltd.
Hillside House, The Square
Forest Row, RH18 5ES

www.templelodge.com

Published by Temple Lodge Publishing 2024
Previous English edition, Temple Lodge Publishing 2010. This new edition has been rewritten and revised throughout

Originally published in German under the title *Die Freie Hochschule für Geisteswissenschaft Goetheanum, Zur Orientierung und Einführung* by Verlag am Goetheanum in 2008. This translation is based on the second edition of 2021

Translated from German by Margot M. Saar. Parts of the Appendix were translated by Marguerite Miller and Douglas Miller for the previous edition of this book

A CIP catalogue record for this book is available from the British Library

ISBN 978 1 915776 16 7

Cover by Morgan Creative
Typeset by Symbiosys Technologies, Visakhapatnam, India
Printed by 4Edge Ltd., Essex

Contents

Preface

This book is an introduction to the School of Spiritual Science, its development and its role today. The new edition aims to present an overview of the School's vibrant history up to and including current activities within its currently eleven Sections. In October 2024 the 12th Section for Inclusive Social Development will be founded. A renewed attempt to describe the spiritual contribution of the individual Sections and their ways of working out of spiritual science forms a central part of this book. Another part focuses on the importance of membership in the School of Spiritual Science and its First Class for the further development and effectiveness of anthroposophy in the life of our time.

The introductory description of the School of Spiritual Science's role and structures underlines the need to direct awareness to what is evolving in human beings and to develop corresponding ways of working, both individually and as a community. This is followed by an account of the diverse motives for membership.

The subsequent chapters address today's ways of working as well as conditions and developments within the First Class of the School of Spiritual Science. The relationship between the inner spiritual work and its application in practice is charted up to the present time. Given the publication in 1992 of the *Esoteric Lessons for the First Class of the School of Spiritual Science at the Goetheanum*, we also look at reasons for and changes to the ways of working that class holders and members have developed together.

An account of the main aspects of the path through the nineteen class lessons leads over to a presentation of the Sections and their specific contributions today to the School of Spiritual Science. As part of this account, Section leaders attempt to outline how the inner spiritual work in their Section relates to and affects the corresponding fields of practical application. Their approaches range from meditation and transformative impulses for daily practice to the forming of communities of responsibility that aim to realize the School's goal of conducting spiritual research. This is followed by a description of the admission process to the School from prerequisites to practical considerations.

The final chapter focuses on the events and different spiritual streams leading from the development of anthroposophy, of the Esoteric School and the first Goetheanum to the founding of the School of Spiritual Science and its First Class during the Christmas Conference of 1923/1924.

The Appendices include all essential statements by Rudolf Steiner on the new foundation and structure of the School of Spiritual Science from 1924 onwards.

In accordance with the School's role as the spiritual heart of the General Anthroposophical Society, this introductory publication is addressed at anyone interested in the School.

As the group responsible for the affairs of the School of Spiritual Science the signees edited the contributions to this book on behalf of the Goetheanum Leadership which holds overall responsibility. Special thanks go to Ariane Eichenberg for her copy-editing.

For the Goetheanum Leadership
Constanza Kaliks, Christiane Haid, Johannes Kühl, Claus-Peter Röh
Goetheanum, January 2024

Recent changes regarding the Sections of the School of Spiritual Science:
Over the past three years the leadership of some Sections has changed. Philipp Reubke (2020) and Constanza Kaliks (2022) started their work in the Pedagogical Section, Marion Debus, Karin Michael and Adam Blanning (2023) in the Medical Section, Matthias Rang (2020) and Vesna Forštnerič Lesjak (2023) in the Section for Natural Science and Nathaniel Williams (2023) in the Youth Section. Jan Göschel will become leader of the Section for Inclusive Social Development.

In 2023 the Sections published the brochure *Insights – Current and Future Research Projects of the Sections for the School of Spiritual Science. goetheanum.ch/en/news/insights-current-and-future-research-projects*

Translator's note:
Works in German referenced in the footnotes are followed in square brackets by a literal rendering of their title in English if no English translation is currently available.

Where an English translation exists but has not been used here, a reference to the available English title is added in brackets.

Wherever an existing translation is cited, only the title and details of that translation are stated.

I would like to thank Jenny Bolsius for her careful proofreading of this translation.

I. The School of Spiritual Science

A School of knowledge of the evolving human being

Constanza Kaliks

The insight that human beings are both earthly and spiritual is central to the School of Spiritual Science founded by Rudolf Steiner at Christmas 1923. As earthly-spiritual beings we continue to evolve. Members of the School of Spiritual Science, in seeking insight in this principle of evolving, draw on future faculties that need to be awakened through spirit-soul activity.

The School's task and effectiveness as an institution therefore lies in uniting two modes of working. On the one hand it facilitates a path of inner development which consists in a quest for knowledge that relies on active, focused interest in the spiritual world and in inner transformation. On the other hand, it seeks to engage with the questions of everyday life and with today's challenges—with the spirit of our time. The knowledge and insights cultivated in the School of Spiritual Science consequently serve the development of a dignified personal and social life. They are the soil on which the corresponding research and tuition can grow.

It was with a view to the quest for insight into what is becoming, into what is of the future, in relation to the world's spiritual reality, that Rudolf Steiner presented, as the content of the School's First Class, a mantric path in nineteen lessons. The continuation of the School to a Second and Third class originally envisaged by Rudolf Steiner did not materialize due to his premature death.

Members of the School of Spiritual Science embark on their quest for knowledge out of their individual initiative in relation to others and to the world. This includes the awareness and recognition that others may have a different relationship to the spirit. Active membership in the School of Spiritual Science therefore relies on the will and readiness to work with others. One condition for membership in the School formulated by Rudolf Steiner is the will to be a representative of anthroposophy. This condition can become a reality when the search for knowledge described here unfolds out of the inner freedom of the individual in relation to others.

According to Rudolf Steiner, membership in the School of Spiritual Science consists in a 'free contractual relationship' between those wishing to become members or co-workers in the School of Spiritual Science and the School's Leadership, represented by individuals assuming responsibility for the School at the Goetheanum. In this way a community can be formed that is based on a culture of agreement and committed to the School's impulse.

Becoming a member of the School means being willing to share responsibility for this institution which has, as Rudolf Steiner said to the members in September 1924, both an earthly and a spiritual dimension. School members therefore form a community of responsibility that aims to carry the work of the School and of anthroposophy in a way that guarantees its existence, development and effectiveness.

Motives for School membership
Claus-Peter Röh

If one asks members, why they joined the School of Spiritual Science they cite very individual motives.

In some, as they face the questions and challenges of our time, grows the wish to actively contribute to bringing about cultural change in the world. The experience of being actively involved in shaping a cultural impulse out of anthroposophy that can protect and promote the dignity of the human being by acknowledging its spirit-soul essence may engender in them the will to assume active responsibility. The question of individual responsibility becomes particularly poignant when one wakes up to the ecological, social and cultural crises of our time and realizes that they demand the urgent development of spiritual approaches and perspectives. In this case, the will to represent anthroposophy not only by absorbing and cultivating it but by assuming active responsibility for it, can result in the decision to become a member of the School of Spiritual Science and its First Class.

Others are prompted by a different kind of motive that is closely connected with a sense of responsibility for the world and related to inner development. Meeting anthroposophy and developing a sense of responsibility for it includes engaging with a view of the human being that assumes a dynamic interaction between spirit, soul and body. When this engagement evokes questions as to our own humanity and new transformative impulses, we may begin to perceive within ourselves, in addition to the person that is of the past, i.e., the person who has become, a 'second' person that is still evolving. A special moment in this experience is the insight that this inner person in us does not appear by itself but requires us to actively bring it about.[1]

The urge to take initiative for one's own further development can enhance the decision to become a member of the School of Spiritual Science. However, this motive would be incomplete without the aforementioned affirmation and active interest in the world and in current events. Connecting both orientations results in a dynamic interaction: the active, transformative interest in the world needs to be carried by individual spiritual training and development. This inner development, on the other hand, needs to be carried today by an inspired, responsible interest in what is going on in the world. Referring to this mutuality Rudolf Steiner described the quality of esotericism as a dynamic relationship between us and life: 'Esoteric life does not consist in our looking down on this or that, and cultivating what happens to please our fancy. It consists in our ability to get thoroughly to grips with life and with the depths of life.'[2]

Depending on a person's biography, their situation in life may provide further motives for membership in the School of Spiritual Science, from the experience that spiritual forces are at work in their daily activities to the wish to enhance these influences and the resolution to embark on a path of inner development.

The experience of destiny and the forming of a community of responsibility

The experience of destiny and of the qualities of destiny in life's events can contribute to the wish for School membership. Again, two interrelated streams come together: faced with certain events and challenges at a biographical turning point, when we are called upon to make an important decision, we may become conscious of the most profound individual impulses. The awareness that in these moments of finding a new direction or taking a decision, spiritual forces were or are at work, carrying this process of transformation, can inspire a sense of gratitude towards them. Experiencing the reality of spiritual forces can give rise to the impulse to enter a conscious path of self- and spirit-knowledge—a further motive for membership.

In his *Autobiography*, Rudolf Steiner contrasted this inner side of experiencing destiny and karma with an external one: 'There are two aspects of destiny that become unified in one's life. One arises from the soul's longing and is directed toward the outer world; the other comes toward a person from the outside world.'[3]

This dual effect of fate requires us to harmonize the two streams in conscious inner dialogue. New spiritual perspectives and ways of acting in the world can arise from the dynamics of this inner duality.

The conscious balancing of external encounters and internal developmental impulses can give rise to yet another motive: the formation of a spiritual community of responsibility that, in ongoing dialogue, enables the perception of experiences; questions and initiatives of other members is a further goal of the School of Spiritual Science and its First Class. As crucial as drawing spiritual inspiration from one's own efforts, work and meditation may be, it is equally essential to share and discuss what one has achieved with a community of spiritual seekers and to be inspired by each other. The search for a widening of this spiritual collaboration is reflected today in the different ways of working employed in the School of Spiritual Science and the First Class. They will be described in the following chapters.

II. The School's structures today

Developments and conditions

Johannes Kühl

The class lessons

In the past, leading personalities within the anthroposophical movement used to view this 'community of responsibility' as a given reality and as a personal inner matter. Members have worked in this sense throughout the past hundred years, first on the esoteric lessons and later, from 1924, on the class lessons.[4] Rudolf Steiner himself appointed several 'mediators' whose task it was to convey the meditations from the class lessons to School members elsewhere who were unable to attend the lessons in Dornach. However, all the 'material' these mediators had were the mantras; they did not have Rudolf Steiner's explanatory texts. When asked about this, his reply was, 'They do not exist', although he himself had agreed to shorthand notes being taken. The reason for this response was his prioritizing of the oral transmission of the School's content. The mediators were therefore required to recreate the mantric situations out of their own active engagement with the mantras for their listeners.

After Rudolf Steiner's death there was some reluctance at first to resume the class work. A few months later and after thorough introspection, Ita Wegman, who had been named as the co-leader of the First Class by Rudolf Steiner and who therefore had access to the texts, began to read them to School members, faithful to Rudolf Steiner's own words.[5] Soon, other members of the School's founding council also began to read the class lessons.[6] After a few years the texts were passed on to further mediators. Because members felt the need to hear Rudolf Steiner's own words, class lessons were always read (class mediators were therefore renamed 'lectors').

A new step was taken in the 1960s and 1970s when Manfred Schmidt-Brabant and Jörgen Smit, two well-known personalities and leaders within the movement, took up Rudolf Steiner's original intention and began to speak freely about the meditations based on their own inner work with them. Soon other mediators followed suit. Conversation groups were also introduced so that by the 1990s three modes of working existed: read lessons, freely rendered lessons and conversations.

The 'conditions' and meaning of class membership today

Rudolf Steiner applied the conditions for membership and for attendance of the class lessons very strictly. He even went as far as excluding members who had put their membership cards on chairs to reserve seats for themselves.[7] There were also stringent rules, set out in the class lessons, concerning access to and passing on of the mantras. Rudolf Steiner warned that the mantras would no longer be effective if they fell into the wrong hands or were made public.

Precisely this happened as early as the 1920s and then again and again throughout the last century. The members nonetheless continued to work on the lessons with great earnestness during the past almost 100 years. In 1991, when the term of the copyright expired and following a series of illegal translations, the Executive Council of the Anthroposophical Society at the Goetheanum and the administrators of Rudolf Steiner's estate (*Nachlassverwaltung*) decided to publish the class lessons. However, because of the long-established approach to these lessons and although they were now published and generally accessible, many members remained convinced that acquiring the texts was 'essentially' wrong because it was not in keeping with Rudolf Steiner's intention.

As the Goetheanum Leadership today we can no longer stand behind this conviction because what has been published is accessible. The mantras may have been much more effective originally, but all members who are earnestly working with them experience their power, richness and depth. There can consequently be no cause for questioning or even abandoning this work. Today many individuals and groups in the world are working with the mantras. The fact that some of these individuals are not School members does not correspond to the intentions explicated repeatedly by Rudolf Steiner in the lessons of 1924.

Given this development we may ask about the meaning of School membership today. Some have become members because they wish to experience the class lessons. But this is not in keeping with the School's intention. As Rudolf Steiner said himself, membership in the School presupposes the wish to become a representative of the anthroposophical cause and the willingness to work together with trust within the School. Esoteric deepening is essential for this. In other words: the School of Spiritual Science is meant to become a community of responsibility for the realization of anthroposophy. This includes taking responsibility for the School as an earthly institution, including its Sections which apply anthroposophy in practice. The publication of the class lessons therefore prompts a reconsidering of the School's intention, which is what we are currently working on.

Groups wishing to work with the mantras should bear this intentional aspect in mind. It may well be that excellent spiritual work is being done in private contexts, contributing to deepening the meditative life of the individuals or groups involved. While this is certainly welcome, it is not necessarily a contribution to the School in the sense described above, because the individuals or groups in question do not seek shared responsibility. Now that the texts of the class lessons are freely available, some groups work on them privately. Others discuss their work with a class holder because they seek to connect with the School, even if the class holder in question is not part of the group. If they wish, the group members can join the School if they are not already members. By consciously sharing in the responsibility, such a group can strengthen the School of Spiritual Science and therefore the anthroposophical movement.

The 'blue card'

How do we deal today with the 'blue card'—the membership card for the School of Spiritual Science—given that the School's content is openly accessible and circumstances are different from when the School was initially established? Some see the card as a 'passport' to the class lessons. This would be unnecessary because people know each other locally and if it was the only reason, it would be a rather superficial one. Presenting the card can also be seen to have a deeper significance: by looking at the card one is newly reminded of the fact that one belongs to an esoteric school that was initiated by the spiritual world through Rudolf Steiner. Having this moment of awareness before every class lesson is a deeply meaningful act. However, there are also groups within the School of Spiritual Science who felt uncomfortable with presenting the card at the door and who have found other forms of admission.

Individual responsibility

From what has been said, it may be apparent that as today's leaders of the School of Spiritual Science we do not find regulations on what 'members may or may not do …' appropriate for our time. By expressing willingness to work together as a community of responsibility for the anthroposophical cause, people take on responsibility and are required to a higher degree to examine their conscience before acting in this context: experiencing the reality of the spiritual world engenders 'humble earnestness'. Regulations may be replaced by the need to seek contact with others with whom one shares responsibility, such as class holders or the Leadership of the School of Spiritual Science at the Goetheanum. Concerning an adequate approach to the meditations, a culture will evolve that one could qualitatively describe as 'esoteric tact'. Feeling connected with the mantras involves not citing them unnecessarily unless the right mood or space has been created for this.

While Rudolf Steiner was able to speak of 'strict rules' out of his own insight, our task today is to either follow these rules based on our own newly acquired insight, or to ask our conscience and act in accordance with a given situation after consultation with our colleagues.

Ways of working in the First Class of the School of Spiritual Science
Claus-Peter Röh

Over the years, different forms of working have been developed in the School of Spiritual Science. When these forms are experienced as arising out of the movement, they can facilitate and protect an essential inner encounter, which means that all class members present contribute to realizing the class lesson and its continually evolving forms.

The 'by word of mouth' principle, which applies to all class lessons, has to newly form in the space where those present speak and listen, trusting in their mutual inner activity. We find the phrase 'by word of mouth' in the Karma lecture of 20 July 1924 where Rudolf Steiner spoke about the seventeenth-century suprasensory Michael School. The unborn human souls participating in that school were taught by the Michael being about the different qualities of script and speech: '... make known what is most important by word of mouth and do not think that only printed books have an effect in the world.'[8] Rudolf Steiner emphasized moreover that it was not a matter of rejecting printed books but of qualifying their importance compared to 'what works in a directly human way'.[9] While it has become possible thanks to printing technology to record contents in black on white and multiply and disseminate them infinitely within seconds, there is also the living word which is carried by the spirit-soul and spoken from person to person. Seeking and developing this in earthly life is an essential task of the pupils of Michael.

Class lessons conveyed in Rudolf Steiner's words
A verbatim-read class lesson uses the introductory thoughts, images and words leading up to the mantric verses as formulated by Rudolf Steiner when he founded the School of Spiritual Science. If these means of conveyance can be transformed into post- and co-creative language, the words

that were spoken in the past can newly invoke the mantric situations. The principle underlying all class lessons takes effect: the speaking and listening community, focusing fully on the mantric content, generates a creative verbal space among its individual members. Many class members and class holders describe how they discover ever new nuances in Rudolf Steiner's introductions as they listen to the read class lesson and experience how it is being built up, gradually leading to and dwelling on the mantric situations.

Freely rendered class lessons

One of the class holders who used to read Rudolf Steiner's words in the lessons for many years was Helga Geelmuyden from Norway. In a letter to Marie Steiner from 1947 she looks back on her work and the questions she asked herself: 'One of the difficulties is that I did not carry out my task as instructed by the teacher, which would have been to bring the class work to life by conveying the meditations based on my own inner engagement with their esoteric content. [...] It may be more correct and beneficial—certainly for the class holder and maybe also generally—if it were done more independently, trusting in the helping powers, as the Doctor had wished.'[10]

Helga Geelmuyden describes a twofold quality of trust that is essential for working in the School of Spiritual Science: on the one hand she trusts Rudolf Steiner and retrospectively also his original instruction to convey the mantric contents as much as possible based on her own inner work. On the other hand, she points to an essential element of the freely rendered class lessons: finding access oneself to the very essence of the mantras rather than from previously absorbed ideas requires brave steps of discovery into the unknown. Growing trust in the helping spiritual powers is essential for these conscious steps of meditation, enquiry, perception and connecting.

In the 1980s and 1990s it was mainly Manfred Schmidt-Brabant and Jörgen Smit who introduced freely rendered class lessons. Now, many groups within the School alternate rhythmically between lessons where Rudolf Steiner's words are read out verbatim and freely formulated lessons.

More ways of rendering class lessons freely are being developed. Some groups have started to hold class lessons as conversations in pairs or groups of three. Experience has shown that this approach to the lesson introduces the challenge of having to raise the quality of the conversation from the level of an intellectual exchange to that of a jointly developed stream. If this is successful, a special intensity of attentiveness can arise among all the individuals involved.

A very recent addition is that all the members present shape the class lesson together. In this case it has been shown to be helpful when the members are prepared and know of this goal beforehand. In the context of a class conference, for instance, this approach would be used at the end of the period of joint study so that all participants can prepare themselves to bear full responsibility together for the forthcoming class conversation.

Forms of School conversation

Developing class lessons as the ones just described based on the efforts of a group of members would not have been possible without the culture of class conversation groups that has evolved over decades. Their growing importance touches the School's living essence in that class conversations can unite different objectives and working levels.

First of all, members can perceive and share each other's impressions of the meditative path through the nineteen lessons and their corresponding tasks and experiences in the spheres of life.

- Cautious conversations about approaching the mantric verses can open new ways of access. An essential aspect of this process is the immediacy of characterizing as opposed to the repetition of fixed expressions from memory.
- A class conversation held before a class lesson can prepare the ground for its effectiveness. When class conversations follow on from a class lesson, members often notice that they feel carried by the previous jointly experienced lesson.
- Because a class conversation group brings together people from one or several Sections and spheres of life, bridges can be built between the School's Sections and the work on the contents of the First Class. In this sense, the forming of a community of responsibility can be reflected in the quality of the group conversation.
- When class questions and themes are carried into life through the week, new questions can inspire and deepen the following class conversations.

What determines the inner and outer quality of the ways of working presented here is the quality of the conversation itself. Experience has shown that the art of a successful class conversation lies in finding the middle between discussing existing, preformed ideas on the one hand and opening to newly perceived essential qualities, contexts and thoughts on the other. Heinz Zimmermann[11] and others have identified conditions for a good conversation culture. Diverse qualities are required to achieve both vibrancy and depth in a class conversation: for instance, a considerate balance between listening and contributing whilst showing the greatest respect for the contributions of others and being particularly awake to the course of the conversation as a whole. When the listening quality in a class conversation is enhanced to an extent that the presence of the theme in the attentive space unlocks new insights, the joint work can approach the quality of a 'spiritual conversation'.

The way in which such levels of conversation can be developed in alternation with the class lessons will inform the School of Spiritual Science's future form and effectiveness.

III. The path through the nineteen class lessons

Johannes Kühl and Claus-Peter Röh

The spiritual essence of the mantric words can be experienced in the process of listening. The following is an outline of the path through the nineteen class lessons.

As we approach the boundaries of the spiritual world from the life of the senses, the 'Guardian of the Threshold' enters our consciousness. This spiritual being has the task[12] to protect us from entering the spirit realm unprepared. The Guardian, a being of truth, rejects anything in our individual development that is illusion or that we have not yet worked through and it guides us with changing instructions through all the subsequent mantras of the nineteen lessons.

As with all mystery schools in ancient times, this School also has written over its entrance the ancient mystery words: 'Human being, know yourself!' The lessons of the First Class lead seekers into situations where they learn to stand before the abyss of their own being: qualities and forces from the past that have become one-sided and rigid in our will, feeling and thinking, appear as shadow images in the shape of three beasts. The devastating insight that we ourselves have brought these hardened counter-images into being can become a motive for us to change and develop the three soul forces for future humanity.

After we have faced the challenge of having to establish and hold our inner balance in different situations through the following class lessons, the seventh lesson takes us for the first time across the threshold into the spiritual world. In turning around and looking back from the spirit realm to our own earthly form and its association with the forces of the four elements, we realize that only in our earthly physicality thinking, feeling and will are woven into one. In the spirit realm they separate into three independent forces. The task arising from this for us is to unite these three forces again out of our own strength as we transition into the spiritual world.

When we reach the middle point of the nineteen lessons, we face a further threshold. As we take the steps of the tenth lesson we are called upon to consciously, by giving ourselves a push, as it were, in spirit and soul, change our inner standpoint: from acting on earth to entering the shining firmament of the stars and beyond to hearing and receiving the spiritual word of worlds that resounds towards us out of the cosmos. This perceiving and hearing of the cosmic forces creates a great triad of relations between us and the spiritual realms around us. This meditative work forms the foundation for the following lessons when the Guardian of the Threshold presents to us the various spiritual beings of the angelic hierarchies. Rudolf Steiner described the work of the divine-spiritual hierarchies in the evolution of the world and of humanity in many lectures and writings.[13] On the path through the nineteen lessons these beings, whose names are taken from esoteric Christian tradition, reveal their presence in the human soul.

The inner support we used to receive from perceiving the four elements of earth, water, air and warmth with our senses no longer holds once we reach the realm of pure spirit. As we continue on the path, the Guardian therefore presents us with the task of meeting the forces of the elements, which now appear differently, with soul faculties that have also been transformed. We must realize in this moment that our speech and actions can be inspired by three beings: the Christ being, volatile Lucifer or hardened Ahriman. In consciously opening ourselves to all three possibilities we can experience a moment of spiritual freedom and take a decision based on these three experiences. The meeting with Christ at this point of the path through the nineteen lessons can be experienced as non-confessional, interreligious, universally human. This threefold encounter finds artistic expression in the sculpture of the Representative of Humanity.

Having experienced these situations of decision-making, we are confronted with the possibility and challenge of learning, in the encounter with the spiritual beings, that the working of the hierarchies replaces that of the elements in earthly life. A reversal or inversion of the will occurs: the newly gained awareness that the three soul forces are an expression of the activities of the hierarchies transforms the purposeful will of earthly 'I' consciousness into a devoted, listening will that is carried by them.

We are then guided in three stages—seeing, listening, creating—to participating in the activities of the hierarchies. In the choir of spiritual beings, the word of worlds resounds and resonates with our own being. This harmonizing of our 'I' consciousness with the spirit concludes the path through the images and inspirations of the nineteen lessons of the First Class of the School of Spiritual Science.

IV. Tasks of the School of Spiritual Science and its Sections

As well as fostering esoteric deepening, the Sections of the School of Spiritual Science represent anthroposophy in public, each Section in its specialist field, and they coordinate their various activities. The work of the Sections aims to vertically permeate the levels of the School which range from the general public to Society membership to membership in the School of Spiritual Science. During the Christmas Conference Rudolf Steiner tried to illustrate this vertical penetration of the fields of practice with spiritual impulses in the following drawing.

The drawing shows how the work within the School could develop. Although the content resembles the content cultivated in the Anthroposophical Society, there is a difference in that the School's content, all of which has by now been published, is conveyed and worked on in a different way. The underlying method includes stages of study and insight that gradually lead beyond material knowledge to perceiving the spiritual world and to acting out of these perceptions. The path through the nineteen lessons and Rudolf Steiner's numerous suggestions regarding esoteric training provide the foundation for an inner development that is not an end in itself but serves to enhance our

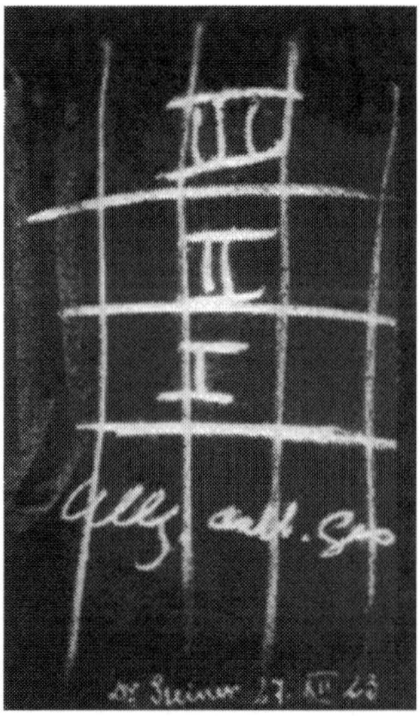

individual effectiveness as we face the tasks confronting humanity today.

Esoteric deepening and Section work

The role of the Section work is consequently threefold: firstly, it supports the striving for esoteric deepening in the professional fields of members wishing to embark on such a path. Secondly, it promotes to the best of its ability global collaboration within the specialized Section fields. And finally, it considers and develops questions and tasks within the different spheres of work and life from a spiritual perspective that is oriented to the human being. As a result, the work in these spheres of activity receives new inspiration:

> Since the School of Spiritual Science cannot be like conventional academic schools, it will not strive to compete with or replace those institutions in any way. At the Goetheanum people will find what they cannot find in conventional universities: esoteric deepening. They will find what their souls are longing for as they search for knowledge. [...] Seekers will find here what they strive for according to their individual life situation. This independent school is not intended to be a purely scientific institution but a purely human one, and it shall fully meet the esoteric needs of both scientists and artists.[14]

Research in the School of Spiritual Science

The School of Spiritual Science is the centre of the Anthroposophical Society's activity. While the Society has the task of promoting spiritual research, the task of the School is that research itself.

As anthroposophy, Rudolf Steiner's spiritual-scientific methods and research results form the basis of the School's work and research. Pursuing a question or topic by consulting all of Rudolf Steiner's corresponding considerations and being inspired by these to reflections and practical applications of one's own can be seen as the first level of anthroposophical inquiry. The next level starts where Rudolf Steiner's spiritual-scientific findings are brought together with the current knowledge in the individual fields of work and in academic research. The work at this level can reach a point where the anthroposophical approach may extend or even remove previous boundaries in specific areas. Conveying this convincingly in public would be a significant achievement.

The next level is that of actual 'spiritual research'. It consists in working meditatively on a question or task over years and can lead to independent spiritual and practical research results. This kind of research naturally encompasses the previous levels.

The following accounts from the currently eleven Sections, composed by the individual Section leaders in 2021, try to describe the inner contribution each Section makes to the School of Spiritual Science. This is not an easy task. Outlines are provided of both the inner goals and tasks of the individual specialist fields and their current practical activities, as far as these can be summarized in such brevity. More information on the individual Sections can be found on the Goetheanum homepage (goetheanum.ch, choose 'School' and the name of the Section from the drop-down menu).

The human being and anthroposophy

General Anthroposophical Section
Constanza Kaliks, Claus-Peter Röh and Peter Selg

The General Anthroposophical Section is concerned with anthroposophy itself, with the essence and development of anthroposophical spiritual science and with the human being as a being of body, soul and spirit. In making the human being its research question and content, the Section develops different directions and priorities that dynamically influence and condition each other. When we join the First Class of the School of Spiritual Science, we embark on a path of inner development and self-knowledge. While this is a path we take individually, it is connected both with a community of responsibility that enables and carries it and with the impact of the Section work in the various spheres of practical application today.

The work in the First Class of the School of Spiritual Science
With the decision to become a member of the School of Spiritual Science, we embark on a path of development and training in the form of nineteen class lessons. Because this path of inner practice describes the spiritual world as a reality of universal humanity, Rudolf Steiner made School membership a task of the General Anthroposophical Section: 'The General Anthroposophical Section will have to be there for all School members.'[15] Having taken the decision to join the Society, many members look for the Section that best reflects their professional interests. The specialized work of the individual Sections has grown widely around the world in recent decades. It can happen today that members are inspired

by their experience of the effectiveness of anthroposophy in a particular sphere of life to seek to deepen this experience by joining the First Class of the School of Spiritual Science.

The starting point for the esoteric path of the First Class is the willingness to create within oneself an open, conscious space of listening attentiveness where the mantric imaginations and situations of the nineteen class lessons can present themselves. As we participate in the class lesson, individually meditating its content, we can come to experience the very essence of the mantras. As our 'I' gradually finds itself in connecting with the spiritual world and the beings at work in it, it may recognize its own cosmic being.

On this path, as we individually meditate on the mantric content, we may develop a growing sense of responsibility for the spiritual forces we experience. This sense of responsibility grows when we share our experiences with other School members. Ongoing efforts to develop forms of working together are consequently also part of the School of Spiritual Science as a community of responsibility: as class holders and members work together, ways of connecting class lessons with class conversation groups have evolved that can rise to the level of spiritual conversations.

As we grow more aware of our spirit-soul being, of our connectedness with others and our embeddedness in the events of our time, we face existential questions: Where does the part of me come from that I recognize as my 'I' and where do I wish to direct my development given the acquired awareness? In his book *Theosophy*, Rudolf Steiner looked at reincarnation and karma in relation to human threefoldness: 'The body is subject to the laws of *heredity*; the soul is subject to self-created destiny or, to use an ancient term, to its *karma*; and the spirit is subject to the laws of *reincarnation* or repeated earthly lives.'[16]

Uniting the experiences gained in individual work with the research of others, including research from public and other study areas, is one of the tasks of the General Anthroposophical Section. This brings up the question as to the method used to gain knowledge and how it can be transmitted. Since Rudolf Steiner developed anthroposophy initially as thought, it is possible to describe and reflect on spirit-soul experiences consciously and closely.

Work research and essential encounter: the development of anthroposophy

Further core tasks of the General Anthroposophical Section include study, publications and events that enable a deepened understanding and inner relationship with Rudolf Steiner's work and inner being and with the development of anthroposophy in the twentieth century, including a relationship with the Anthroposophical Society and its history. Developing a profound 'cultural memory' of Rudolf Steiner and the developments he initiated both internally and in public is a crucial aspect of the School and its Sections.

The spiritual essence of anthroposophy lives in the esoteric lessons of the First Class. The teachings of these lessons belong, both historically and spiritually, to the Michaelic and Rosicrucian community. The General Anthroposophical Section develops and promotes studies and initiatives that cast more light on these contexts and allow individuals to relate to them in differentiated ways. In addition, it conducts and promotes research into the destiny of the Anthroposophical Society and its members, their life work and legacies. These endeavours lead to the building of a spiritual community of which individual members can feel that they are a part. Cultivating a connection with anthroposophists who have passed away is as much a task of the General Anthroposophical Section as identifying the intentions of foundations initiated by Rudolf Steiner and his co-workers that continue to form the basis of the School's Sections today.

> Infinitely much would be gained if this selflessness could take hold in the world so that those who live later would connect with the dead and consciously try to maintain continuity in evolution. No matter whether it is a purely elective affinity, or any other kind of kinship brought about by karma: connecting with those who are trying so hard to send the pure rays of their influence out of the spiritual world is immensely important, particularly if we embrace this consciously.[17]

Additionally, the General Anthroposophical Section conducts and promotes the study of central anthroposophical themes and concepts such as freedom and karma, the hierarchies, Christology or the forces and powers of evil; it examines these topics in Rudolf Steiner's life work with a view to their relevance to the specialized Sections today, from medicine to education, from agriculture to economics.

Another of the General Anthroposophical Section's responsibilities—work research and essential encounter—is connected with the Rudolf Steiner Archives and the edition of Rudolf Steiner's complete writings and lectures (GA) which is still not complete. New publications bring ever more nuances to the foundations of anthroposophy, of the Anthroposophical Society and the School of Spiritual Science.

Studying anthroposophy

The study, communicability and reception of anthroposophy belong to the foundations of spiritual-scientific insight. Insight into emergence, life and metamorphosis relies on active reception which requires individual engagement and experience.

Striving to understand the human being in relation to the cosmos, to others, to oneself as an evolving being can enliven, inspire and transform this relationship. This search for knowledge as active participation in reality poses challenges that transcend the acquisition of knowledge. The General Anthroposophical Section therefore seeks to promote ways of actively receiving spiritual science, to examine, develop and practise spiritual science in interaction with individuals, institutions, professional fields and training centres. The study of anthroposophy as such can, in this sense, form the beginning of spiritual-scientific inquiry: because it strengthens independent thinking and judgement as an expression of the 'I' on the one hand and, on the other, attempts to make this thinking so receptive that it can find access to the reality and essence of others. The study of anthroposophy is consequently not only preparation but can in itself fulfil the mission of the School of Spiritual Science.

Through repeated practise on the meditative path of the class lessons, the unfolding of the human 'I' can be deepened into knowledge. The search for an encounter with one's own essence and with the spiritual reality aims to guide our interest in the world and in others towards a growing sense of commitment and connectedness. As we study spiritual science, we create the cognitive foundations for this: a conceptual form that makes it possible to permeate the emergence and essence of a spiritual reality with the light of consciousness and to shape our lives accordingly.

Around the world and at the Goetheanum, the School of Spiritual Science strives to create spaces where this way of gaining knowledge can be practised.

For current activities and plans visit www.goetheanum.org/allgemeine-sektion.goetheanum.ch/en

Youth Section

Constanza Kaliks (Section leader from 2012 to 2023)

The Youth Section is a place where young people can give expression to their questions, intentions and searching in encounters, projects and initiatives. Young people try to find themselves and their own way in life in relation to others and to the time they live in. The Youth Section aims to create opportunities where young people can express the intentions, expectations and hopes that live in them but that they are initially unable to formulate.

Often it is this attempt to give expression to the ineffable that opens up a space where a will is discovered that points to and is connected with the future. 'For young people today, being young exposes the longing for spirit',[18] is how Rudolf Steiner summarizes this relationship with the ineffable. The Youth Section's content and goal do not consist in a 'programme' but 'it will attempt to allow life to arise from its young founding members' sense that something is missing'.[19]

'The only thing that stays the same is that we keep changing.' This is how a young person once described the underlying feeling of their generation. In a society where transition, the preliminary itself, is constant,[20] being young is a dual challenge. Jobs, working contexts, relationships become increasingly transient projects of shorter or longer duration, meaning and orientation become a permanent challenge. Where then does what we do imprint itself? Where does it leave its traces? This question as to the relevance of one's own being in connection with others often arises in an existential and distinctive form.

A recent major research project within the Youth Section illustrates just how concrete and distinctive such questions are. The guiding question in this three-year project concerned the role of the will in young people's searching: 'What would the world look like in 2030 if what lives within you becomes a reality, and what will you do to make it happen?' What can each of us do so their contribution is imprinted in the course of the world? The research findings reveal that living with this question and dealing with it in dialogue is what can draw the future into the present and make our connection with what lies ahead more concrete.

The Youth Section's work draws from ever new sources: every project, every new initiative offers the young people involved the chance to connect with their own intentions. It is a becoming aware of the encounter between an inner effectiveness that unfolds in the world and the destiny that approaches the individuality out of the present time and its specific challenges.

This attentiveness that is at the same time perceptive and creative in the relationship between the 'I' and the world can be practised. In the experience of their encounter, a sense of being one with the world can arise and grow into a feeling of connectedness that makes living with the big existential questions possible.[21] A feeling of belonging can emerge, a sense of hope and of future that can pave the way for an understanding and experience of the humanity of others. This connectedness can also inspire the search for a deeper understanding of the longing for the spiritual dimension of reality and of one's own path in life.

As young people transition from the third to the fourth seven-year period, they awaken to the possibility of actively participating in the world. This can express itself in their growing awareness of their own destiny, in their quest to find their vocation, in their question about inner, meditative work. The search for active participation in the world in relation to one's own inner life can take many different forms that are not mutually exclusive and that often change in the course of adolescence. A determined commitment to social challenges and causes can be as important as a meditative life. The field is one of encounters where—just as on the mantric path of the class lessons—the 'I' can form itself in connection with the world and the world in connection with the 'I'. The spirit can be experienced as an individual reality that is formed in relation to others and that alters, connects with and assumes responsibility for what has come into being as a result of this relationship. Rudolf Steiner saw youth as a spiritual-scientific discipline that was to have its own Section in the School of Spiritual Science. 'Spiritual Science exists for souls who want to wake up. It attempts not only to convey knowledge but also to make life accessible, to free people to transform life into knowledge.'[22]

This kind of active listening, inquiry and commitment are alive in the Youth Section today, in conferences organized by young people for young people, in working groups, colloquia, research projects and publications—in a living network that connects young people around the world.

For current activities and plans visit www.youthsection.org

Developing our humanity in medicine

Medical Section

Matthias Girke and Georg Soldner (Section leaders from 2012 to 2023)

Developing a spiritual-scientific medicine and promoting the necessary research, tuition and practice are among the Medical Section's key tasks. The Section aims to meet the growing needs of patients and to provide a medicine that has the human being at its centre. Mainstream medicine today is in danger of increasingly mechanizing diagnosis and therapy, of limiting the therapeutic relationship and of formalizing its therapeutic practice with a guideline-oriented approach. Based on scientific medicine, Anthroposophic Medicine seeks to develop a quality in healthcare that takes into account the whole human being, body, soul and spirit. This asks for a spiritualized medicine that is both professional and ethical. Connecting the two is intrinsic to the concept of the School of Spiritual Science in that its meditative path of knowledge is linked to practical patient care and all other fields of work within the Medical Section.

The esoteric work in the Michael School coalesces with the Section's research, science, tuition and practical application of Anthroposophic Medicine, Anthroposophic pharmacy and other therapeutic professions. The Michael School's meditative path of knowledge and the Section's scientific and practical endeavours unite in a way that is characteristic of the School of Spiritual Science and that distinguishes it from the profile of conventional universities. On the one hand, the effectiveness of the meditative work relates to an individual ethical and spiritual development that aims to guide the spirit in us to the spirit in the universe.[23] This is the path of the Michael School and its worldwide community of responsibility. On the other hand, the meditative work unfolds its effectiveness also in practice, making the human soul receptive for the right inspirational thought at the right time. Medicine is more than a professional specialty concerned with evidence-based effectiveness only: it also has a moral dimension that requires consideration of every person's uniqueness. While the 'right' thought always presupposes a corresponding effort, there is always something of a grace in every good idea and, in a certain sense, it is often a longingly awaited gift. On the School of Spiritual Science's meditative path of knowledge and with the specific meditations for physicians and therapists the soul can open to the spiritual world and 'learn to listen' out for helpful inspirations. The meditative work also proves fruitful in the development of therapeutic relationships. The soul becomes able to truly empathize with others and to sense something of their destiny. And lastly, the meditative work can enhance the therapeutic forces. The meditative path of knowledge therefore unites with practical life.

The healing effect of spiritual development within the School is deepened further through the subject-specific meditations. Immediately after the Christmas Conference of 1923/1924 Rudolf Steiner developed a path of knowledge especially for physicians[24] and—we can say today—also for therapists. This medical meditative path deepens the connection with the healing forces of the plant world and nature realms. Based on an esoteric experience of the elements this path opens up a deeper understanding of health and sickness in patients and shows the way to the patient's healing forces and need for healing. The Michaelic meditative path is complemented by the Raphaelic dimension of healing. While the Michaelic path leads to the spiritual essence, allowing it to also shine through in the sensory experience, the Raphaelic path enhances the healing forces. There is an essential connection between the light of knowledge and the life unfolding in healing, in that life forces metamorphose in the human organism into the light forces of thinking. But the reverse is equally true: the light of the spiritual world builds up the human life forces and body. When we wake up, life is transformed into light; when we sleep, the archetypal images of the human form work into the organism's life processes. Light and life are then transmitted by warmth. The heart is an organ that releases a wealth of warmth, gifting it, as it were, to the world. In warmth, the human 'I' becomes effective and the spirit unites with the natural world. Morality connects with nature through warmth. This is why one of the central meditations, the 'Warmth Meditation,' starts with the question, 'How do I find the good?',[25] evoking not the scientific but the moral dimension of medicine. The therapist's esoteric training encompasses both the School of Spiritual Science's path of knowledge, which is shared by all the Sections (the Michaelic path of the School's First Class, in other words) and the Raphaelic meditations which enhance the therapeutic healing forces.

For current activities and plans visit medsektion-goetheanum.org

Developing our humanity with nature

Natural Science Section

Johannes Kühl (Section leader from 1996 to 2020)

In every organism, the whole is reflected in the individual organs where it is directed towards a particular task. The same is true for the organism of the School of Spiritual Science and its Sections. The School's overarching motive of connecting esoteric deepening with practical life shifts in the natural sciences in that the search for knowledge itself, rather than its immediate effect, constitutes its practical activity. Once the natural-scientific findings prove to be fruitful in therapy, farming etc., we have already reached the next step where the working together of the Sections becomes relevant.

What kind of esoteric deepening can scientists look for in their professional work? This is a great challenge given that the 'scientific conscience' needs to be observed on the one hand, which means that we should refrain from speculation or unrealistic effusiveness. On the other hand, we need to keep an open mind, however convincing the materialistic view of the world may be. Scientific thinking, or the 'scientific conscience', is therefore fundamental to anthroposophy and present to a greater or lesser degree in all Sections. 'Natural Science is therefore the true basis of vision today.'[26]

Initially, any new phenomenon or relationship we discover constitutes a kind of spiritual experience. This sensation passes quickly, however, once the new discovery becomes knowledge. A 'good' scientist will discover something about themselves even at this stage: what awakens my interest? Where am I superficial? Where do I hold on to familiar ideas? How can I be open to new things?

The Goethean science we pursue in the Section relies on exact sensory observation as a way of connecting directly and intensively with nature—with a plant, for example. Reflecting on the metamorphosing leaves, for instance, makes us recreate this process inwardly and connect more intimately with the processes of life and growth, but also with those of death. Wherever this is not possible, such as in some areas of physics, we need to carefully develop an awareness of the conditions leading up to a phenomenon in order to get to know its 'contextual field' through variation of these conditions. The idea we generate in us as we do this can be deepened in meditation and lead to an imaginative understanding of the context in question.

Or take the process of observing a landscape or a particular location over the course of the year. As we encounter and inwardly pass through the different stages of the year—the germinating in spring and dying in autumn, the different weather conditions—we can feel how we inwardly connect with this landscape as if it was a living being. The term 'genius loci' describes this aptly. Such exercises can deepen our relationship with the rhythms of the year and the way we work with Rudolf Steiner's Soul Calendar. In addition, they enhance our awareness of current perceptions and experiences which can gain significance for our individual destiny.

In the lessons of the First Class of the School of Spiritual Science we learn to experience how our own being—the one we call on when we say 'Human being, know yourself!'—cannot be found in this beautiful, rich, mysterious and sometimes also threatening world of the senses. The more intensively we face this question, the more the observations and objects around us move to the background and disappear from our inquiring mind. It is as if the world was shrouded in darkness regarding this question. Only by experiencing this void will our inner eye be opened for the second darkness that veils the spiritual world at first. Natural scientists, who know the value of the sensory world better than anyone, struggle particularly at this point. However, the more conscientiously they pursue their goal, the better they know how to be honest and sober and how to cultivate the 'scientific conscience' mentioned earlier. These skills need to be taken along on the path; they even need to be enhanced, as a form of love for the truth. Only then can we approach an authentic spiritual experience that is safe and right for our time. We realize the importance of this conscientiousness in the natural sciences for spirit knowledge even before we reach the threshold. The subtitle Rudolf Steiner chose for his book *The Philosophy of Freedom*—'findings of introspective observation following the methods of natural science'—summarizes this with exemplary concision.

There are consequently two aspects to esotericism in natural science: on the one hand a deepening of the relationship to nature and the interrelations we discover and intellectually grasp there, which are always spiritual. On the other hand, it requires an enhancement of the scientific faculties so that the spiritual world can be experienced realistically and thus even more intensively.

The path of inner development aims at deepening this experience. The difficulties of scientists who are oriented to the sensory world are transformed into helpful tools here. 'Where knowledge of the senses ends'[27] is something every scientist becomes aware of with every research project; for instance when they fail to find a formula for the way the purity of the prism spectrum touches them, or when the blue butterfly on the bright yellow flower awakens a sense of awe in them that exceeds their premise of giving a detailed account of the butterfly's life and habitat.

Mindful observation as well as clear and consistent thinking are the two pillars of natural science. More than anyone else, scientists may have experienced the gift and grace of witnessing laws and ideas in their relation to the sensory world not only in a finished form but also as they emerge, that is, in their 'preconceptual' state. Unconditional openness to the world and the readiness to actively devote to mobile thinking without restrictions are faculties which immensely promote the meditative life and work.

For current activities and plans visit www.forschungsinstitut.ch

Section for Mathematics and Astronomy
Oliver Conradt

The Section for Mathematics and Astronomy encompasses two polar but mutually complementing areas. There is mathematics on the one hand, which relies on thinking. The mathematical will to think can grasp the logic of abstract concepts and use them to create inner images and representations. Surprisingly, the ideas formed within the human mind correspond in certain cases exactly to the natural laws of the physical world. On the other hand, there is astronomy which begins with the sensory perception of the starry skies. The cosmos with the earth and the human being is its object of observation. Questions as to cosmic evolution and our relationship as human beings to world evolution arise naturally. This polarity in itself can inspire in us the wish for meditative deepening, which is also called for variously in the class lessons of the School of Spiritual Science.

Mathematics, now divided into multiple specialized areas and often highly abstract, impacts on many spheres of life today through the sciences, technology and economics. While mathematicians experience the various, clearly delineated, specialist fields as attractive, clear and useful in practice, others tend to see the subject as impenetrable and daunting. The basic questions of astronomy, a very comprehensive field, are in danger of seeking answers either in the materialist and abstract images of astrophysics or in the interpretations and directives of astrology, which are hardly accessible to the thinking mind.

Mathematics based on anthroposophical spiritual science strives to kindle new life in the abstract, logical and systematic thoughts and to connect with and experience thinking in a living way. At the level of living, imaginative thinking, the principle of polarities in projective geometry and the augmentation in the metamorphoses that convey those polarities play an essential part. The images and ideas created are not only important because they depict something but also because they are formed from concepts using the soul's powers of imagination. At the level of inspirative thinking the experience of concepts—algebraic concepts, for example—widens and becomes inner hearing. We no longer experience the concepts as solely our own products, but they reveal their own being, their 'own tone' within the life of soul. The 'I—numbers' in mathematics belong to the cognitive level where a spiritual being no longer only experiences itself as being but can face itself like a stranger.[28] Rudolf Steiner introduced the term 'I–number' in relation to supra-imaginary numbers.[29] There are approaches today by various authors who view quadri-quaternions, Clifford algebras or projective algebras as examples of I–numbers.[30]

Spiritual-scientific cosmology relies in the first place on phenomenological astronomy. If we can perceive the cosmos, the planetary system, the earth organism, the earth being and our own essential humanity from the periphery, we also change how we relate to our actions. We will experience a growing need to let other people, other beings, the world around us come to life in everything we do.

Lastly, the Section for Mathematics and Astronomy is also devoted to teaching and teacher development. Experiencing the potential of one's own will to think and the beauty and clarity of mathematics on the one hand and the human relationship with the entire cosmos on the other are important aspects of adolescence.

For current activities and plans visit www.mas.goetheanum.org

Section for Agriculture
Jean-Michel Florin and Ueli Hurter

Biodynamic agriculture arose from questions posed to Rudolf Steiner about the future of farming, the earth and nutrition. Biodynamics which is widespread today around the world evolved from only eight lectures Rudolf Steiner gave in June 1924. In these lectures he placed particular emphasis on the need for a spiritual understanding of nature and especially of farming activities. 'Given that our life depends on what the earth provides, agriculture in particular makes apparent that we need to draw on spiritual forces if physical human life on earth is to continue.'[31] What Rudolf Steiner anticipated a hundred years ago has become uncomfortable reality today. The current ecological situation calls the continued existence of humanity and of the earth into question. The inclusion of the spirit is an existential requirement today.

Paths to the spirit are always individual, but these different paths can meet and this is how a vibrant biodynamic movement has evolved in the past hundred years. Biodynamic initiatives have emerged across four generations, on all continents, in all climates and cultures. On every farm, this spiritually extended agriculture incarnates in a particular way. Every biodynamic farm is consequently a potential 'site of spiritual research'. The agricultural practice and reflection on this practice yield ever new research questions for farmers. In addition, consultation, training, research, processing and marketing have evolved. New questions keep coming up that require spiritual deepening, questions that form the living substance of the Section work where we distinguish three key areas:

How can I find an approach to living creatures on the farm that suits their nature?

Inquiry into a sustainable and dignified way of dealing with soil, plants and animals has become a burning issue. As a first step, we need to wake up to this question and feel the need of these beings. The resulting genuine concern, which can be truly painful ('My animal is suffering—what can I do about this?'), can make us more attentive and mindful, and as a result we can gradually approach a spiritual dimension that can open up when sense-based observation and the understanding derived from it meet a boundary. We need to be attentive in our daily activities to moments when we come up against this boundary of the sense world in space and time. Can we pause there? Can we catch a glimpse into life's spiritual dimension?

Farming offers many opportunities to meet this boundary and gradually awaken to it: in the 'threshold moments', when the relationship between the sensory and suprasensory worlds changes: when an animal dies or is born, for instance, when we are sowing or harvesting, when substances are transformed in the composting process, or when the entire farm being achieves a balance over the years and decades.

There are also many moments when our actions are no longer carried by a causal logic but by precise intuitive evidence. We reach a spiritual level in our very actions: in milking, in stirring the biodynamic preparations and so on. Reflecting on these moments can help us deepen these experiences.

These research questions flow into the annual theme of the Section's big agriculture conference at the Goetheanum that seeks to inspire ethical and sustainable ways of working. A social space is created for dialogue on research. Using various interactive methods, we try to find new insights together that everyone can then implement in their work. The spirit, the essence, emerges as we interact, as we struggle for knowledge together.

The following statement by Rudolf Steiner refers to the collaborative quality we are looking for:

> When people let their feelings shine together of their own free will, this creates something which again goes beyond the purely emancipated human being. The emancipated human being has an individual soul; this will never be lost once it has been gained. But when people come together voluntarily, they group around focal points and this gives

> opportunities to spirits to act like a kind of group soul but in a very different way from the group souls of old.[32]

It is always a wonderful experience when a group of people working together develops the feeling that something new, something more than the sum of their individual contributions, is emerging from the future. Rudolf Steiner also describes how these beings leave us free:

> In the past, group souls used to make us unfree. But these new beings allow us to have full freedom and retain our individuality. We may even say they draw their existence from our unity. It will depend on human souls whether or not they give as many such higher souls as possible the chance to descend to humankind. The more groups are formed and the greater the sense of community that is created in complete freedom, the more sublime beings will come down to us and the sooner our earthly planet will be spiritualized.[33]

Can I as an individual farmer pursue a path of inner development?

Opportunities for personal deepening are plentiful in the work of a farmer and even include simply walking through the fields. Rudolf Steiner says that farmers are 'in fact meditants [...] You walk across a field and suddenly there it is—an insight that you then try out in practice.'[34]

The daily course, the yearly cycle, the movements of the stars, they all offer much scope for esoteric work. Farmers can deepen their connection with the rhythms that carry life between heaven and earth both qualitatively and meditatively. The weekly verses of the anthroposophical Soul Calendar can help them in this.

Many farmers appreciate Goethean science with its precise phenomenology at the boundaries of space and time as an important developmental path that can lead them to the spirit in nature. In the lessons of the First Class of the School of Spiritual Science we are called upon as individuals, irrespective of our profession, to take responsibility and calmly and without fear walk the path into the spiritual world of our own free will. In some imaginations of the class lessons, motifs that are essential to agriculture, which lives between earth and cosmos, can be found again in different ways, creating a bridge to the farming practice.

Another indication by Rudolf Steiner—that farmers can 'easily become clair-sentient in their sense of smell'[35]—reveals a further field of spiritual research in farming. As a farmer I experience ever-changing moods on my farm by perceiving them, often unconsciously, in the atmosphere. I can for instance smell as soon as I enter the barn when there is a sick animal. This faculty needs to be developed further so that I get better and better at sensing the consequences of actions in the atmosphere and have deeper encounters with the being of nature.

How can I assume responsibility?
How can I carry the spiritual reality into the material world so as to find a better foundation for my concrete agricultural activities and act consciously and responsibly out of insight?

In the last fifty years, the individual and joint study of Rudolf Steiner's Michael Letters has come to form the Section's spiritual backbone.[36] These texts which constitute a condensed form of anthroposophy, are like a legacy of Rudolf Steiner's who introduced them as a starting point for individual work. If we can unite our work on these letters with our own experience, their content can become like a seed from which much can grow. The activity of Michael, the spirit of our time, is described and juxtaposed with that of Ahriman. Michael never forces us to take any particular action because he respects our freedom. Connecting with Michael can become inner experience. The final letter—*From Nature to Sub-nature*—for instance helped us deepen the topical question of the digitalization of agriculture.

This work can give inspiration and strength for our daily tasks wherever we are on earth and for the global challenges of our time, particularly in the field of agriculture and nutrition.

For current activities and plans visit sektion-landwirtschaft.org

Developing our humanity through art

Section for Performing Arts
Stefan Hasler and colleagues

In what way can performers such as eurythmists, musicians, speech artists, actors and puppet players seek esoteric deepening in their professional field? Or, to put it differently, where do our artistic practice and activities take us? In what field of forces does this search unfold? And the next question: What inner steps help us to shape our daily professional life?

We can say that every discovery, every way of dealing with a phenomenon or a new situation are spiritual experiences. It is just that these moments quickly disappear again from our consciousness and what used to be new becomes something we know. It is at this stage that artists can make the first discoveries about themselves: What awakens my attentiveness? When am I too superficial? How do I achieve deepening? Where am I caught up in familiar feelings? How do I open myself to new things? How can meditation help us prepare for our work?[37] How can Imagination, Inspiration and Intuition become tools for me in my endeavours? For which professions did Rudolf Steiner give specific meditations?[38]

Such diverse questions require a variety of responses, which is why we will let several colleagues speak for their professional groups:

Puppetry

> The union of the visual and performing arts in puppetry enables viewers to find a way to imaginative vision by means of the figures that are brought to life. As I give life to these figures as a puppeteer, my soul is transformed into a 'devil' or 'angel', for instance, and I can achieve the same transformation in the viewer. [*Mathias Ganz*]
>
> According to the German writer Heinrich von Kleist (1777–1811), puppets are closer to god than human beings. They are the opposite of infinite consciousness. But they are a medium and behind them stands a person, awakening them—godlike—to life. Doing justice to this challenge does not only require technique but also profound empathy and willingness to learn. The means recommended for honing these skills are daily meditation, a thirst for knowledge, courage and openness to new things. After all, wise kings, innocent fools and wicked witches are waiting to be effectively represented. [*Christa Horvat*]

Music

> Not only the works of brilliant composers but even individual musical elements such as intervals have much more width and depth than what lives in our conscious soul. Esoteric questions therefore arise almost naturally for musicians because the comprehensive sphere of music is a mysterious spiritual essence. It can lead us to experience how any endeavour to bring earnestness and responsibility to this essence also helps to open up new musical horizons. [*Christian Ginat*]
>
> 'To experience music consciously we need to experience it anthroposophically,' Rudolf Steiner said[39] of the intimate connection between music and anthroposophy. If we permeate music with consciousness today, we can connect with the old stream that saw the essence of music unfold in the triad of *musica instrumentalis*, *musica humana* and *musica mundana*. We can find the essence of our humanity reflected in the mirror

of the musical works and elements, the evolution of human consciousness reflected in the history of music and in the diverse musical cultures and tonal systems. As we develop active, creative listening, we prepare in ourselves the ability to be inspired. This ability can be further developed and become spiritual hearing, in other words, the experience of hearing spiritual beings that the mantras of the School of Spiritual Science ask for again and again. Musical research within this School has above all the task of demonstrating the spiritual bridge from everyday consciousness to music's and humanity's spiritual home in the Devachan. [*Matthias Bölts*]

Speech and Drama

As a speech artist I experience daily how poetry—artistic texts—makes it possible to say the unsayable. They can make something happen that raises me far above my everyday self, something that diversifies and deepens my soul experiences. In speech I am looking for esoteric deepening in the language and effect of the mantras. Can I be mindful of how an image, a phrase, the metric form and rhythm of words, lines and verses contribute to letting the mantra become a gateway? Can I learn to hear and shape how an esoteric being speaks to me and where from, and what layer or region within me it reaches and moves? How can the cautiously searching movement of a group of people become a vessel for something to happen? For me, the work of the School and the Section mean to live spiritual science. [*Agnes Zehnter*]

In their artistic training, speakers and actors seek to connect with the word's Logos forces. They sense that they could not realize their humanity without the word, without speech. This means that many of the elements of practice on this path of development are esoteric in themselves. They include training in Greek pentathlon, using the surrounding air as a sounding board (hearing oneself from the outside), dealing with the forces of sound, rhythms, gestures that live both in speech and in the moving human being as well as the grammatical structures of language. [*Silke Kollewijn*]

The Mantras of the nineteen class lessons guide us from image to image. The language is spiritual-dramatic, severe and poetic. Its effect is both emphatic and intimate. We understand as we listen and awaken to the living experience of being connected with the world of creative spirit beings. This awareness is painful. The language of the Mystery Dramas is taken from the same spiritual source. It, too, is poetic through and through; the thought is imbued with will. The scenes of these plays illustrate how we develop when we live with the class lessons. They illustrate how life unfolds when it is filled with the content of the class lessons. The drama of the spirit is revealed in these four plays. The protagonists are karmically connected with each other. The individual's quest for knowledge reveals where someone can walk in freedom or where karma needs to reign. We awaken to each other in the encounter. The spirit world connected with this turns the present experience into a moment of timelessness that offers space to both the past and the emerging future. Powerful drama that expects entirely new techniques of actors because everything becomes speech. In my experience, the two enlighten and enhance each other. [*Catherine Ann Schmid*]

Eurythmy

We eurythmists work with forces of uprightness that we did not use up as children when we learned to walk and that were therefore internalized.[40] With eurythmy I seek to find out where these forces come from, what kind of beings they are and how they affect us. As well as in specialist literature, I find the most effective help with this in the words of the class lessons as long as I am prepared to work on them meditatively. Questions regarding thinking, feeling and will, the rhythms in eurythmy gain great significance—as do the elements that are at work in me and in the world, the speech of the gods, the Logos that affects us through the sphere of the zodiac and the planetary movements. I can experience how every word that I turn into consciously guided movement out of my life body is a new birth. These meditative experiences help me to understand why every eurythmy movement is at the same time a questioning, listening and speaking and why inner movement is required for me to comprehend these texts. [*Maria Scheily*]

One of the first basic questions for me as a eurythmist is how I can perceive my whole self as an instrument. Am I convinced that I consist of body, soul and spirit?[41] If I am, it soon becomes clear that my feet connect me with the earth, my middle with other people and my head with the cosmos.[42] This confronts me directly with the basic question as to whether I seek to connect to the spiritual reality with each eurythmy movement I perform, whether I am open to this spiritual reality and whether such a connection will really be achieved. This threshold situation is always present. The threshold that needs to be crossed is sometimes smaller and sometimes wider. [*Stefan Hasler*]

Each professional group has its own field of practice and therefore its own 'gateways' for becoming aware of the spiritual world. The question is directed inward, to our own soul life, and passes through the soul to the spirit. With every new challenge it is therefore connected with the fundamental human question, with the call: 'Human being, know yourself!'

This call is also the basis of the esoteric work in the First Class, which is interdisciplinary and not restricted to a particular profession. The daily artistic practising on and with one's own soul life, which assumes that my own feelings can also be experienced as the place where other beings are at work, the self-observation and simultaneous activity are essentially very close to meditative experience. With the right inner attitude, the daily practice can also become a way of practising meditation. Imagination, Inspiration and Intuition then become gateways to the spiritual reality that can be unlocked with a tone, a sound, a movement, an image. This is what people strive for in the most diverse configurations around the world.

For current activities and plans visit srmk.goetheanum.org

Humanities Section
Ariane Eichenberg and Christiane Haid

'... for we become what we are through our words'.[43]

The Humanities form a bridge between art and science. While scientists start from the universal and look for laws that link individual phenomena, artists embody out of their individuality the law intrinsic to each work of art, creating something special in each case. Scientists try to find a way to the spirit through matter, while artists shape matter out of the spirit. The Humanities unite and interweave these two approaches. In the intersecting movements an inner space emerges for observing one's own activity. The overall context, the necessary mutual dependency of knowledge and artistry, becomes apparent.

'The connection with the spirit is severed if it is not perpetuated by beauty. Beauty connects the "I" with the body.'[44] Beauty, which is here presumed to be the uniting element and therefore a holistic experience, encompasses both truth and goodness and aims consequently at the depths of existence. Beauty in this sense means the coincidence of inner and outer and is always whole, always holistic.

In the Humanities beauty appears as word. This appearance ranges from linguistic means of expression to the mystery of the Logos. Language and the word create coherence and demand transformation.

The word belongs to both body and spirit and weaves in the soul space in between. We need the physical body for speaking; we inhale the air of the cosmos, individualize it in our blood and exhale it in a depleted state. Dead matter is transformed into audible sound—forces of resurrection are at work. The word is not merely a means of outer expression, but its formative forces work back on the organism in our breathing and blood. At the same time our speech with its organs takes hold of the spirit and the surrounding cosmic space. Our breathing rhythm connects us with the sun, for it reflects the macrocosmic rhythm of the Platonic year. The word, carried by our breath, can become the element that can make us aware again of this connection. In immersing ourselves in the ocean of words we engage with the spirit of language and seek for ways of making the unsayable sayable again. If we are successful, the world comes to life, becomes Logos: '...It is alive in us, our true being, streaming out of our soul life; we ourselves are it [...] Out of it the divine beings speak to us, the Logos.'[45] Mantric language is Logos. As we connect with it in practising, we experience ourselves increasingly as cosmic beings.

The stages of higher knowledge—Imagination, Inspiration, Intuition—can be experienced in an archetypal way when art and science come together. The imaginative character of language becomes visible as image and gesture; at the level of Inspiration, the interaction between microcosmic and macrocosmic events becomes audible through rhythm, sound and relationship, so that the beings reveal themselves as creators in the next step at the level of Intuition. Science conducted in this way is artistic, and art that embraces this kind of consciousness is scientific. This dual movement can only be developed and experienced dialogically, in the community—it is mutual transformation. The School of Spiritual Science, the Michael School, provides the space for this path.

For current activities and plans please visit ssw.goetheanum.org

Visual Arts Section

Christiane Haid

'Creating forms as an expression of inner life' Rudolf Steiner

Referring to his new artistic impulse, Rudolf Steiner said that developing a form of artistic activity that instils in the observer a new kind of thinking as an experience of a spiritual reality was the ideal of the Visual Arts Section. The effect on the perceiver of artistic presentations and architectural designs arising from this approach is comparable to meditative experiences. The difference is that the means used by the artist aim to create a sense-perceptual phenomenon while meditants work at the spirit-soul level. The substance thus formed can lead directly to spiritual experiences. It is therefore a logical consequence that Rudolf Steiner devoted the second phase of his development of anthroposophy to the visual arts and to drama, speech and music. Art in this sense refers to the relationship between creating art and receiving art, as part of which the artists make available to the observer a form that inspires a spiritual movement in the latter. Creation and perception of the creation are therefore interdependent and a work of art is only possible when the two enter into a relationship. Rudolf Steiner calls this new approach to art a 'key point in the current progress of human evolution'.[46]

The buildings, sculptural forms, drawings, graphic and painting work created by Rudolf Steiner are mostly a reflection of cosmic laws. An example of this is the metamorphosis of the capitals in the first Goetheanum representing Earth's planetary evolution. The window images for the first Goetheanum, carried out by Assya Turgenev for the second Goetheanum, are motifs of human and world evolution. And the group sculpture depicts the two opposing powers with the figure of the Representative of Humanity at the centre, holding the balance. What these works have in common is that they are not about the artist's personal expression but depictions of spiritual laws and beings. They are an attempt, one could say, to express through the arts what is at work behind the sense-perceptible phenomenon. They do not seek to present spiritual visions in the form of images or symbols but are rather like a musical score that only achieves its true purpose as a work of art due to the observer's active involvement. Engaging with these works does consequently not involve interpretation or divination but a possibility for spiritual movement actively seized as a step towards spiritual experience. It means:

> entering into things and joining in the process of creativity that came from the higher hierarchies and fills and forms the whole of our world. There is no need to avoid doing this just because it is more difficult than symbolic or allegorical interpretation, because it leads into the spiritual world and is the very strongest incentive for truly achieving imagination, inspiration and intuition. [...] For the realms unlocked by this contemplation hold the elements which will make our world whole again and which will lift us above mere maya to true reality.[47]

The anthroposophical art impulse, whilst using different means, pursues the same goal as the path of the nineteen mantric groups of the First Class. It also strives for the higher stages of knowledge: Imagination, Inspiration and Intuition. Both paths enhance each other, for in many of his introductions to the mantras Rudolf Steiner used blackboard drawings to swiftly outline and visualize the situations evoked by the meditations. Art is used here to show how closely and essentially connected artistic means and expression are to the path of the nineteen lessons and how it can enhance and deepen its effect.

The connection of science, art and religion, which was still alive in the old mysteries, is equally fundamental to the School of Spiritual Science as an institution dedicated to the founding of the new mysteries. The difference today is that we need to establish this connection consciously. As the central element, it has the crucial task here of carrying 'the spiritual-divine life to the earth on the one hand and to upgrade earthly physical life so that its forms, colours, words and sounds can appear as an earthly revelation of the spirit'.[48]

Access to the spirit is not simply given to us today but finding it is a developmental task. The path through the nineteen lessons can be an essential aid in this and enrich the artist's creativity.

In the Visual Arts Section, we aim to combine both directions: carrying the divine-spiritual life to the earth to the extent this is possible for individual artists and shaping the artistic means of the individual genres so that something 'unearthly' can appear through them.

The artistic work of individuals within the Visual Arts Section can therefore not remain purely personal biographical expression, but the task is to provide research fields and questions that we work on together within the Section.

For current activities and plans visit sbk.goetheanum.org

Developing our humanity in the social sphere

Pedagogical Section

Florian Osswald and Claus-Peter Röh (Section leaders from 2010 to 2020)

Rudolf Steiner's pedagogical impulse aims to develop innovative approaches in education that recognize and include spiritual forces at work in human beings and in the world. This aim leads those active in Waldorf Education to look consciously for boundaries and thresholds of experience.

The first threshold experience arises for educators when they develop the thought that children bring their own individual impulses with them from a spiritual life before birth. This thought leads to a central task of education: to match these spiritual life impulses with the child's mental and physical development in a way that allows them to unfold healthily. This inner attitude changes the way we look at education in that our daily perception and actions are imbued with new forces of respect, mindfulness and interest as we meet and interact with the children. At the next level, we can ask for help from the spiritual forces that participate in the education of children and young people as angelic beings. The 'Teachers' Imagination',[49] given by Rudolf Steiner, describes imaginatively the relationship of educators to their personal angel. The uniting and inspiring influence of the archangels helps to raise the individual to a communal relationship, for instance in building up collegial collaboration. When a whole school community courageously devotes their decisions and actions to working together in today's world, they may, in special moments, sense or experience the creative, intuiting effect of the archai or Spirits of Time. This inclusion of spiritual forces in education leads to a third threshold experience. As child and teacher meet as whole human beings, resonances in soul and spirit may be evoked. When educators work on their personal transformation, the learning child's being, which also strives for transformation, can take inspiration from this inner buoyancy. In turn, educators who keep working on themselves will be able to sense and understand the dynamics of child development more deeply. Self-development and the experience of the threshold of one's own spiritual essence are therefore part of the teacher's professional esotericism. Directly after founding the school in 1919, Rudolf Steiner therefore gave the teachers their first meditation, which guides the polarity of sense experience and thinking process towards an enhanced human self that finds new access to the spiritual forces in meditation. Four years later, following a pedagogical crisis, the teachers were given a second professional meditation which also follows the principles of polarity and enhancement: out of the tension between spiritual and bodily existence, this second meditation takes a transformative step towards the creative, constructive power of the higher human self.

With the founding of the School of Spiritual Science at the Christmas Conference of 1923 and the subsequent establishing of specialized Sections, new perspectives also opened up for the spiritual deepening of Waldorf Education. On the path through nineteen lessons and mantric groups, esoteric pupils see themselves in new inner situations and experiences of soul and spirit. In experiencing the immediate presence of spiritual forces, they can build within themselves the confidence that they will be able to act in perceptive and transformative ways in their pedagogical encounters.

The thoughts developed in the Anthropological Foundations (GA 293) of the First Teachers' Course are expanded as we live through the imaginative pictures and situations described in the lesons of the School of Spiritual Science. Thoughts and descriptions are permeated by experiences and sensations arising as we work and live through these imaginations. Cosmic forces and beings connected with our will impulses can gradually begin to shine through.

The threefoldness of the soul forces (thinking, feeling and will) and of the human organism (head, torso and limbs) form the basis of Waldorf Education and its method and of the path through the nineteen class lessons. This proximity of content gives rise to research questions in the Pedagogical Section. Following the spiritual-scientific method of 'approaching something from different sides and then combining the different aspects into one comprehensive view',[50] the two paths are brought together in studies and conferences, where one of the class lessons is worked on in different ways, while a topical educational issue is studied on the basis of the Anthropological Foundations. If the building up of both aspects is successful, the participants can experience themselves as both creative and perceptive in the emerging tension between the imagination of the class lesson and the pedagogical question. Unexpected phenomena and relations often emerge from the perceptive and questioning activities between the two sides. Everyday pedagogical experiences can become easier to understand and deal with when viewed from these different perspectives. As one newly reflects on and formulates these transformative moments, one often experiences amazement and reverence for the imaginations of the School of Spiritual Science and for the wisdom of the living pedagogical practice. Realizing the questioning and research processes described involves the constant further development of ways of working together. Developing new qualities in meetings and conversations is crucial when educators and teachers come together for this kind of work—in colloquia or events of the Pedagogical Section or in the corresponding meetings in the various countries: the greatest respect for the experiences and descriptions of others; careful weighing up between listening and the impulse to make a contribution; awareness of the transformation of content in the course of the conversation; awareness of the entire course of the meeting from the beginning to the consciously shaped conclusion; cultivating a conscious looking back and looking ahead to the future.

The experience of this quality of conversation can approach that of an insightful conversation as the individual achievement is raised to the inspirational space of a community that listens and seeks further development. This trust in the human encounter is akin to the spiritual essence of education, which aims to discover in the encounter what is striving to become in the individual child or young person.

For current activities and plans visit www.goetheanum-paedagogik.ch

Section for Social Sciences
Gerald Häfner

Finding appropriate ways of shaping the social sphere has become a question of human survival. While in ancient times humanity and society were guided by an outer wisdom, we have to guide ourselves today. What once used to be left to a few initiates or a few individuals who were chosen and prepared for their task by destiny, now falls to each of us individually. However, we need to develop and practise the ideas, forces and skills required for this self-guidance.

Anthroposophy can bring living thinking to the usual representational thinking and help our abstract, isolated consciousness to connect with living forces and beings. This can be experienced in the class lessons and applied in practice in the work of the different Sections and corresponding spheres of life.

Rudolf Steiner gave specific meditations and esoteric indications for teachers, priests and physicians, but not for the wider social sphere. One reason for this may be that social questions today are not seen as concerning specific professional fields but an almost unlimited number of professions and, in a deeper sense, even each individual person. We can therefore take the entire anthroposophical path of inner development, with all the indications we have regarding content and method, the meditations and inspirations, as the Section's esoteric content and working material. The path of the Michael School and the class lessons play an essential part in this in that they can contribute to the transformation and extension of the soul forces and therefore to a deepening and transformation of our relationship not only with the physical, enlivened and spiritual world but also with ourselves.

Steps on the path through the nineteen lessons include practising the ability to detach ourselves from our everyday consciousness and learn to look at ourselves as from the outside. The next step consists in gradually transforming our own soul faculties of thinking, feeling and will as a prerequisite for opening ourselves to the spirit that lives in, around and above us. As we gradually perceive, by expanding our usual horizon, different, more comprehensive, spiritual views of the world and of our life, our perception of social realities and potential for action can also grow, and we may develop a new, enhanced sense of social responsibility.

The Section for Social Sciences receives important inspiration from Rudolf Steiner's basic works,[51] essays[52] and lectures[53] as well as from laws, thoughts and maxims he formulated for the social sphere in particular, such as the 'social archetype',[54] the 'basic maxim of the free human being,'[55] the 'fundamental sociological law'[56] and the 'main social law.'[57] Additionally, he created verses and mottos that have a special connection with the social sphere, including the 'motto of social ethics' which he gave to Edith Maryon on 5 November 1920: 'The healthy social life is found / When in the mirror of each human soul / The whole community finds its reflection / And when in the community / The virtue of each one is living.'[58] These inspirational works not only form an essential basis of study for the Section, they also often describe ways of inner, social and spiritual practice to be fostered individually, and in certain contexts also communally, within the Section.

The social aspect as an inner and outer path of development

As well as every true encounter, all social, economic, juridical and political processes have an esoteric dimension, but there is no protected field of experimentation. Everything we try, think or do is a reality and has consequences. The soul and the world are the laboratory of our endeavours. The social life is neither a workpiece we can simply produce nor is it something we can think out or conceptualize. It arises through, with and among us. It is a path of development that we walk together and that requires, concerns and encompasses all our soul faculties: thinking, acting, and particularly the middle sphere of feeling.

We also realize that the social life has become something like an educational path in our time. Others become a gateway for us to learn about ourselves and about the world. Only together can we develop ourselves and find our impulses and tasks in the world. This educational path in the social realm is one we have to take. It becomes increasingly clear and urgent that this path needs to join and complete the anthroposophical inner path of genuine self- and world knowledge.

We all have questions such as: Should we change the world or rather ourselves? Do our hearts need to change or the circumstances? What seems to be an often heatedly discussed contradiction, we in the Section see as an inseparable whole. Separation would render the achievement of our goal impossible.

Bravely shaping the future

Public life today is increasingly determined by different qualities of fear: fear of infection, of climate change and global warming, of environmental destruction and the loss of species, fear of terror, war and civil war, of displacement and foreign domination, fear of a brutalization of the political culture and the decline of democracy, fear of surveillance and control, of decline and poverty—tremendous deep-seated fears of the future.

And yet: 'We can only overcome the fear of a future we dread with images of a future we want.'[59]

The Section for Social Sciences seeks to juxtapose the fear of the future with a vision of the future and the sense of powerlessness with the power of social insight and creativity. It hopes to achieve this by viewing the social life itself as a path of development and by developing learning paths that can transform fear into courage, both through individual inner work and by working with the imaginations of the class lessons. In order to achieve this, the Section encourages and supports concrete initiatives that work towards a different world and a more humane society. We are working on developing positive, encouraging, strengthening images of our shared future within a growing global network. Our practical work includes concrete impulses for developing democracy, a free and solidarity-based economic order, a new approach to money, reformed property law, appropriate leadership and management, and for peace and conflict research and social work.

For current activities and plans visit www.sozial.goetheanum.org

V. Membership—Study—Contact

Johannes Kühl, Claus-Peter Röh

Conditions and implications of membership

Members of the Anthroposophical Society can join the *School of Spiritual Science* by taking the decision to become a class member and obtaining confirmation from the School's Leadership at the Goetheanum. This personal decision, as well as expressing an intention of future activity, also confirms a discovery made regarding oneself.

As the previous contributions illustrated from the most diverse perspectives, this membership is about an individual living relationship with anthroposophy as a path of knowledge, as a spiritual concern rooted in the present. Once someone has discovered that anthroposophy can become a part of their life that they would like to commit to, they may develop the need to deepen this relationship. The decision to embark on the path of the First Class with its nineteen lessons first raises this relationship to anthroposophy to full consciousness and then allows for a connection with forces that support the development of faculties in relation to knowledge, the social sphere and life in general.

Engaging with the situations of the nineteen class lessons is, as Rudolf Steiner once pointed out, not the motive for membership in the School of Spiritual Science but rather a consequence of the decision to become a member. School membership consequently results from a personal decision and the affirmation of its consequences which could be summarized in the following way:

> the wish to represent anthroposophy in life;
> the wish to work with others on initiatives and the advancement of knowledge;
> the wish to lead a meditative life, gain self-knowledge and achieve self-transformation.

As well as these inner aspects there is also an outer condition: membership in the Anthroposophical Society. When discussing the Statutes of the Society Rudolf Steiner proposed a membership in the Anthroposophical Society of around two years before admission to the School could be granted. However, he himself did not always adhere to this proposal. What is, in fact, required is sufficient knowledge of anthroposophy and of the Anthroposophical Society for someone to arrive at an informed decision.

The practicalities of admission

Today, the process of becoming a member is as follows: one finds a School member locally and has a conversation with them. Generally, such a contact person or mediator can be found locally in a professional context or branch of the Anthroposophical Society. Contact details can be obtained in local publications, from the branch office or knowledgeable anthroposophists; alternatively, there is always the option of contacting the Goetheanum. Members of the School faculty at the Goetheanum and some of their co-workers can also be contacted regarding School membership.

This initial conversation is mainly about getting to know one another and obtaining clarification on the various aspects of membership. Membership is the foundation of collaboration which means that both sides need to be able to affirm this collaboration and take it seriously. The mediator is the human connection, as it were, with the community of School members and the Goetheanum Leadership.

The second step consists in writing a letter to the Leadership of the School of Spiritual Science at the Goetheanum. This letter should, if possible, be handwritten and contain a short biography, an outline of one's relationship with anthroposophy and details such as age and the date of joining the Anthroposophical Society. It should also contain confirmation that one has read this publication and that one acknowledges the ways of working outlined in it. This letter is handed to the contact person who will send it on with their own endorsement to the School's Leadership at the Goetheanum. The Leadership will then issue a membership card that will be forwarded to the applicant via their contact person. The applicant is then a member of the First Class of the *School of Spiritual Science*.

Members of the School of Spiritual Science are not only members of the First Class but also of the General Anthroposophical Section. This Section's main concern is research and deepening of general anthroposophical questions on the one hand and the development of the skills needed for anthroposophical work on the other.

Beyond that, active involvement in the specialist Sections can be sought for professional or subject-specific reasons. There is no formal admission or membership card for the Sections; membership is simply based on personal interest and a commitment to collaboration. All Sections offer events, work groups and meetings for School members, where subject-specific and professional questions are worked on in connection with the anthroposophical path of knowledge. Inspiration for Section research, conferences or publications arises from these events.[60]

As illustrated in the previous chapters, the *School of Spiritual Science* at the Goetheanum is not an alternative university but sees itself rather as a living environment of responsibility where research, teaching and consultation complement what is offered by universities, colleges and similar institutions. It is a space where professional development and spiritual deepening are at the centre, a space for a holistic approach to science, the arts, religious and social questions. All the Sections are active worldwide.

Contact:
School of Spiritual Science
at the Goetheanum
Nicolas Criblez
Rüttiweg 45, CH-4143 Dornach, Switzerland
Phone +41 (0)61 706 43 64
schoolmembership@goetheanum.ch
www.goetheanum.org

VI. History and foundation of the School of Spiritual Science

Christiane Haid

The School of Spiritual Science's foundation at the Christmas Conference of 1923/1924 was preceded by almost 20 years of inner preparation. In the Statutes of the Society Rudolf Steiner mentioned his intention to establish three classes within the School of Spiritual Science. He pointed out that there had been three such classes before in the form of three work groups or Sections of the Esoteric School that existed from 1904 up until the beginning of World War I in the summer of 1914. Some essential motifs of their work are outlined below.

Western esotericism and cognitive science

When in 1902 Rudolf Steiner agreed to become general secretary and therefore head of the Theosophical Society's German Section, it was essential for him to emphasize that his access to the suprasensory world was rational-scientific. Rudolf Steiner viewed thinking as a process which generates a new consciousness that enables us to connect with the world. The initial constitutionally caused separation between the 'I' and the world can be overcome as we connect perception and concept in thinking.

In drawing on Goethe's cognitive approach and on German Idealism as a central-European philosophical tradition Rudolf Steiner represented an independent spiritual direction of Western orientation. He developed the central aspects of his spiritual science in the first phase of his involvement with the Theosophical Society up until 1909: a Rosicrucian epistemology that included the evolution of the world, the essence of the human being, the anthroposophical path of inner development, Christology and the idea of reincarnation and karma to name but a few. They were not derived 'from old traditions', he explained, but he had researched and presented them 'out of the immediate awareness of the present time'.[61] Spiritual knowledge was not to be an end in itself, serving only one's personal development, but weave into life and be fruitfully applied in education, medicine and other contexts.

A 'School of Spiritual Science'

When in 1911 the impulse for a building dedicated to the performance of Rudolf Steiner's Mystery Dramas was born,[62] the leaflet of the *Johannesbauverein*,[63] an association founded especially for this purpose, mentioned the possibility of a 'School of Spiritual Science' for the first time. However, the leaflet does not only speak of a building for theatre performances but describes how the building initiative holds the seed for the later School of Spiritual Science: 'The School of Spiritual Science will take up the academic knowledge capable of development that has been allowed by its official representatives to turn rigid with materialism and will elevate it to spirit knowledge, guiding it into the temple where its union with art and religion will facilitate the living mystery.'[64]

The union of science, art and religion corresponds to the kind of understanding of the world that used to live in the ancient mysteries, where human beings shaped their lives in harmony with the gods and based on an all-encompassing view of the world and the cosmos. It is the aim of spiritual science that modern human beings with their intellectual-scientific approach to the world reconnect with the divine-spiritual world. The experience of the spirit can inspire the way they shape their individual and social life. Human beings can gain a wider understanding of the whole of culture and civilization as they connect with nature, the cosmos and the spiritual world which is the source of everything. This wider horizon can help them to achieve a form of knowledge and way of life that respects the world and all human beings equally.

The first Section of the Esoteric School 1904–1914[65]

In 1904, Rudolf Steiner established an Esoteric School for members wishing to deepen their theosophical work individually and who were looking for an independent experience of the suprasensory. In doing so, he continued the impulse of the Esoteric School founded by Helena Petrovna Blavatsky.[66] Since 1902, Rudolf Steiner and Marie von Sivers had been members of that school, which was by that time led by Annie Besant. In 1904, Rudolf Steiner began to hold esoteric lessons himself in his capacity as general secretary of the Theosophical Society's German Section.[67] In 1907 he parted amicably from Annie Besant's school and pursued an independent path based on Christianity and centred around the Mystery of Golgotha.[68]

Under the title 'General criteria those wishing to undergo esoteric training need to set themselves'[69] Steiner gave his students, whom he also accompanied personally, 'six subsidiary exercises' and other meditations. Once work in the Esoteric School had started, he also published a series of essays in the magazine *Lucifer Gnosis*[70] on 'How to know higher worlds'. The series was published in book form in 1909.[71] Interestingly, the last chapter of this book is on the Guardian of the Threshold, the same motif that appears at the beginning of the class lessons in 1924. In the book *How to Know Higher Worlds*, the basic principles of the Rosicrucian training path were presented publicly for the first time, making the methodical foundations of spirit knowledge accessible to everyone.[72] Basic motifs on this path of esoteric training are soul exercises that cultivate and deepen the human capacity for perception and thinking. Embarking on this path can give access to the realities of higher worlds and their cognitive and moral conditions. Based on the exercises described one can get to know the deeper layers of reality.

Membership in the Esoteric School required an invitation from the School Leadership. Unlike the central esoteric training book, the School's esoteric work was not publicly accessible nor was it known at that time.[73] Around 800 members attended the Esoteric Lessons. With the beginning of World War I, Rudolf Steiner closed the School because under the circumstances it was no longer possible to work in groups that were not accessible to the public.

The second Section of the Esoteric School 1904–1914

Prompted by questions from members Rudolf Steiner gave several preparatory lectures in 1904[74] which led to the founding of the Esoteric School's second—'Cognitive-Ritual'—Section. Some of these members used to be active Freemasons and were now looking to work with symbolic acts similar to the masonic rituals. Again, Rudolf Steiner followed the law of continuity[75] by building on existing masonic traditions, in this case the Memphis-Misraim Rite founded by John Yarker, a form of Egyptian High-Degree Masonry to which Helena Petrovna Blavatsky was also connected. Freemasonry is in fact related to the craft of the mason: the activities in the lodge symbolize active achievements outside the temple. It was from this work that the architectural impulse of anthroposophy and anthroposophically inspired art evolved.

The Cognitive-Ritual Section[76] had around 600 members. Like the Esoteric School's first Section, it also ceased to operate when World War I broke out and for the same reasons.

There is no information on the third Section although it is mentioned by name. It seems that the members adhered strictly to the obligation to secrecy that applied to the Esoteric School at the time.

The laying of the foundation stone for the first Goetheanum—a cultural impulse enters the world

In the evening of 20 September 1913[77] the foundation stone was laid for the first Goetheanum in Dornach near Basel/CH. The underlying intention was to give new spiritual impulses to culture in response to 'humanity's yearning call for the spirit' that resided unspoken in every human being.[78] The Goetheanum was to be the place where the connection with the spiritual world would form the foundation and inspiration of active life in every field. With the Dornach building up and running, anthroposophy was for the first time visible in the world. After World War I the first activities and initiatives evolved in the various spheres of life. The Waldorf School was founded, as were hospitals, medical practices and homes for people with special needs. Initiatives arose for social renewal through threefolding of the social organism. There were attempts to change the academic educational system by students and academics in cooperation with Rudolf Steiner.

As these activities increased, they also became increasingly superficial in the 1920s, a development that Rudolf Steiner observed with growing concern. Some institutions failed, particularly in the economic context. The so-called 'academic courses' (*Hochschulkurse*),[79] an initiative for the renewal of the academic system, remained unsuccessful and made many enemies due to the clumsy and offensively dogmatic way anthroposophy was presented in public. In addition, there was much tension between younger and older members who had different ideas on how anthroposophy should be conveyed and realized.

The New Year's Night of 1922/1923 saw the destruction of the Goetheanum by arson. Rudolf Steiner said that the ruin of the building was an external expression of the Anthroposophical Society's inner state: the members had devoted themselves so entirely to practical activities that they had forgotten about anthroposophy and its need for continuous cultivation. The crisis caused by this neglect[80] led Rudolf Steiner in 1923 to initiate intensive social processes in order to achieve a thorough rethinking and reorganization of the Anthroposophical Society.

At a deeper level, both the need for restructuring the Anthroposophical Society and the intentions to found the School of Spiritual Science were due to the developmental situation of humanity today and its relationship with the spiritual world. This relationship and the way it is shaped have to do with the nature of human thinking and with the effect of Michael, the spirit of our time. A few aspects of this very comprehensive topic are outlined below.

Michael as the inspiring influence of our time

In 1907 Rudolf Steiner began to speak of the Archangel Michael[81] as the being inspiring the present age. He did this first in the Esoteric Lessons[82] and later on, from May 1913 onwards,[83] also in his lectures to members in London and Stuttgart. Due to Michael's activity a new revelatory stream became accessible to humanity out of the spiritual world. Christian tradition depicts the Archangel Michael as the dragon slayer. As the defeater of the dragon, he is both an image for and an imagination of the supersensible being of Michael described by Rudolf Steiner, to whom he assigned a much more comprehensive and significant mission than Christian tradition had done. According to Rudolf Steiner, Michael has been the reigning and inspiring spirit of our age since 1879 and his reign will last 300 years in total.[84] Michael's mission is the administration of cosmic intelligence, that is, of the supersensible substance of thinking[85] which is directly connected with the all-encompassing primal ground of the world. When we think, we connect our perceptions with concepts and rise—consciously or unconsciously—to the world of ideas where, through our individual activity, we see the concepts as spiritual form.

With the beginning of his reign, Michael takes on a particular task for the following 300 years as the spirit of time, a task that is related to human thinking. At the end of the nineteenth century cosmic intelligence had arrived on earth, which means that since then thinking has been available to us human beings freely and is no longer guided by divine spiritual beings or worldly authorities. Michael guided this cosmic intelligence as it entered the human soul, endowing us with ever greater freedom and independence. We can now use our thinking freely and for our own ends on earth, without relating to any spiritual reality. As a result science, technology and the economy have developed since the late nineteenth century at a previously inconceivable rate. At the same time much of the natural world surrounding us has been destroyed leading to immense crises in many areas. The human conquest of the world, the exploitation of nature and its resources, social inequality, wars and environmental damage reflect the fragmentation and isolation that are the result of our disconnection from the spiritual world. Our task today is to develop a new kind of awareness that we are one with the world and to act accordingly.

Through self-knowledge we must learn to understand the spiritual nature of our intelligence and become aware of its cosmic origin. From the spiritual sphere, which is adjacent to the physical world, Michael accompanies this process of growing freedom, waiting for us to take the initiative so that he can come towards us and inspire our thinking. Human intelligence, if it loses sight of its cosmic origin and therefore its wider context, is in danger of being used solely for material purposes. Whether we can perceive this cosmic origin, in other words, whether we can consciously grasp the ideal foundation of the world depends on whether or not we will be able to stand up to the ahrimanic powers whose goals are purely materialistic and whose dragon-being seeks to distract us from the spiritual world and chain us entirely to the earthly, material world. In this struggle with the dragon we are accompanied by Michael, who has been known for centuries in Christian tradition as the dragon slayer. However, because Michael will not restrict our freedom, he never interferes of his own accord but waits for us to freely take the initiative to gain knowledge of and consciously connect with the spiritual nature of the world.

The Christmas Conference of 1923/1924[86]

The Christmas Conference stands for an entirely new beginning in the history of the Anthroposophical Society and the idea of a School of Spiritual Science. While Rudolf Steiner had up until then only ever been a teacher and not even a member of the Anthroposophical Society, he decided at that time to take on the presidency himself and appoint an executive council. Together with the council members he would assume responsibility for guiding the Society and the School of Spiritual Science. The Executive Council members were therefore appointed both as leaders of the Society and as heads of the School's individual Sections.

At the Christmas Conference, Rudolf Steiner and around 800 members consulted and decided on new Statutes for the Society. In addition, Rudolf Steiner presented a series of spiritual-scientific lectures[87] on the destiny underlying the emergence of the Anthroposophical Society. This lecture series formed the beginning of the 'Karma Lectures' that were soon to follow. The spiritual symbol for the foundation of the Anthroposophical Society was the Foundation Stone Meditation, which Rudolf Steiner conveyed to the members during the ceremonial founding act on 25 December 1923.[88] In parallel to the physical foundation stone sunk in the earth in 1913, the Foundation Stone Meditation could and can be sunk by each member into their heart in verbal, meditative form, guiding them in association with the Trinity and the Hierarchies on the path of becoming human.

The School of Spiritual Science as Michael School

Anthroposophical spiritual science teaches an approach to knowledge and science suited to our modern consciousness. It can help us to find a way to the spiritual world of our own initiative and independently. The Goetheanum as a School of Spiritual Science sees its task in supporting its members in developing and deepening this path to knowledge and science.[89] Opening to the spiritual world is an original impulse in the individual human being. However, as indicated earlier the spirit of time, Michael, perceives and accompanies the individual person in this because of his special relationship to the development of cosmic intelligence. Michael is therefore the spirit of time that inspires and accompanies the School of

Spiritual Science in spirit; his teachings were conveyed by Rudolf Steiner in nineteen class lessons. Deciding to become a member of this School consequently implies the wish to become a pupil of Michael as the spirit of time and to be willing to take active responsibility in the cultural mission of spiritualizing civilization.

When Rudolf Steiner founded the School of Spiritual Science, he consciously united two aspects that had until then been seen as separate: his conveying of spiritual knowledge on the one hand and an institution devoted to earthly organization and administration on the other. Rudolf Steiner said this was a risk he took in relation to the spiritual powers but that he found that these spiritual powers had accepted it, as was apparent in the developments after the Christmas Conference. Rudolf Steiner's activities in the year and a half leading up to his death reveal a major stream of spiritual inspiration that found expression in the Karma Lectures[90] and in countless courses for other spheres of life, such as the Agriculture Course, the course on Education for Special Needs, the Drama Course and the Apocalypse Course for priests, to name but a few.

In the Karma Lectures Rudolf Steiner described in a unique way Michael's direction of a suprasensory school in the spiritual world in earlier centuries. In their life between death and a new birth, those connected with anthroposophy prepared themselves for incarnation in the twentieth and twenty-first centuries by learning about the development and destiny of cosmic intelligence in order to be able to bring Michael's teachings to life in their new incarnation. The *Michael Letters*, which Rudolf Steiner started publishing on 17 August 1924 and continued right up to his death on 30 March 1925,[91] are aphoristic descriptions of these events, their purpose and effect.

In taking this step, Rudolf Steiner created a challenge but also an opportunity that continues to this day: to shape and take responsibility for anthroposophy's suprasensory reality as a spiritual movement down to its embodiment in earthly social forms. This means that individually received inspirations do not only remain thoughts but become deeds.

Six weeks after the Christmas Conference, on 15 February 1924, Rudolf Steiner began with the first lesson in the Michael School's first class, the first so-called class lesson. By the time he fell ill in September 1924, he had held 38 class lessons in Dornach and other cities, completing only the first section of the first class. In contrast to the Esoteric School, the existence and goals of the School of Spiritual Science were mentioned in the General Anthroposophical Society's public Statutes and some of its content was even described in the members' Newsletter.

The three classes

The Statutes of the General Anthroposophical Society mention three classes of the School of Spiritual Science. Rudolf Steiner was unable to establish the Second and Third Class in his lifetime but indicated in the nineteen class lessons how the work could continue: the second section would have described the imaginative pictures of the suprasensory cultus[92] from the beginning of the nineteenth century. The teachings of the suprasensory Michael School during the fifteenth, sixteenth and seventeenth centuries would have been the subject of the third section. In the Michael Letters[93] and Karma Lectures Rudolf Steiner gave indications as to the direction this would have taken. This concludes this brief outline of the School of Spiritual Science's background and history. A list of recommended reading for further deepening is attached.

APPENDICES

Texts by Rudolf Steiner

Below are basic texts by Rudolf Steiner on establishing the School of Spiritual Science. They are taken from GA 260a: *Die Konstitution der Allgemeinen Anthroposophischen Gesellschaft und der Freien Hochschule für Geisteswissenschaft* [The Constitution of the General Anthroposophical Society and the School of Spiritual Science]

The Organic Development of the Anthroposophical Society and its Future Tasks

Dornach, 18 January 1924

In the second Newsletter—as you know this Newsletter is called 'What is happening in the Anthroposophical Society'—you will find an address I gave to the Members. Allow me to read the opening sentences to you:

'The Christmas Conference for the Foundation of the General Anthroposophical Society must not be restricted to the experience of members attending it at the Goetheanum. The conference will only come to full realization wherever people who are devoted to anthroposophy feel that the inspirations radiating out from the conference have engendered new anthroposophical life. Without that, the conference would not have achieved its purpose.'

There is no doubt, my dear friends, that the Anthroposophical Society needs new life. What took place here at Christmas needs to be seen as incomplete. The Christmas Conference will have to be continually nurtured by the future activities within the Anthroposophical Society. In the past such conferences were essentially considered complete in themselves; at most, people remembered them as an experience they had in the past.

This Christmas Conference is different in that it was not conceived as a passing event. It had a specific content and character. If you reflect on it, you will find that it had something that came directly from the spiritual world. We tried to break away from the usual administrative nature of such gatherings and instead let the spirit shine through in every single detail. As I often said before, the spirit has its own laws and they are different from the laws of the physical world. Let us consider the spiritual background of the Christmas Conference and how the individual activities in the Anthroposophical Society have grown out of this conference.

If we regard the Christmas Conference as we did previous conferences, it will gradually disappear and its content will be lost. In that case it would better not have taken place at all. The spirit tends to vanish if one does not hold on to it. It does not disappear from the cosmos but from the place where it is not nurtured and it finds another place in the cosmos. Something like this Christmas Conference does not rely on earthly events. Don't think that the impulses of this Christmas Conference, if they are not fostered, will go away and appear somewhere else on earth. They do not need to. They can find refuge in entirely different worlds. Everything therefore depends on our commitment to the Christmas Conference and on our internalizing of its content. The Newsletter for members will make this possible.

The first issues of this Newsletter will reflect on the events of the Christmas Conference but also on the will that lived there. We will build on this will. I will start with this in the second Newsletter and continue in the following issues. What is important now is to look back on what used to live in the Anthroposophical Society and to look ahead to what ought to happen in the future.

Let us begin by looking back from this vantage point and by creating a framework for the Christmas Conference. The Anthroposophical Society started very, very small at the beginning of the century and as part of the Theosophical Society. How was that? We can really disregard the Theosophical Society, for what evolved as the Anthroposophical Society grew organically from its own source, from its own seed. Originally, there were only very few people in the Anthroposophical Society. They gathered in small groups in various places. Public events were also modest. Except for the members who were actively involved in the Society no one was really aware of the anthroposophical movement in those early days. It was wonderfully peaceful when the world did not yet take notice of anthroposophy. It only lived in the consciousness of those who came together in the anthroposophical groups. Among them were people who sought to connect the innermost needs of their soul with anthroposophy as it streamed from the spiritual world. More and more of them gathered and formed what would become the Anthroposophical Society. Those who were unable to connect the needs of their soul with it stayed away. Initially, these were simply people who were not interested, who did not get particularly upset but who said: 'What they have to offer is not for me' and they stayed away. We were able to do our work in peace and guide those seeking for higher truths towards these higher truths in the smaller gatherings.

This initial situation was only outwardly disrupted by the war. Moving between the different countries was of course no longer possible in the same way as before. The global tyranny of the war prevented more intimate meetings, but the true spiritual stream that has always flowed through anthroposophy was always there.

However, anthroposophy does not only concern individual people and their needs of soul; it concerns human life in general. Wherever a creative human impulse seeks to become effective, this creativity can connect with the source of anthroposophy because anthroposophy concerns humanity as a whole. We were soon able to make a start in Munich with an artistic endeavour.

This artistic endeavour—the performance of the Mysteries—meant real inner progress for some people as they were able to see as pictures what they had absorbed before through the ideas into which the spiritual life had been poured. The peaceful development of anthroposophy was not really disturbed yet by this performance of the Mysteries in Munich. We experienced some hostility here or there but not enough to cause us concern, for in esotericism it is best to work positively, out of the immediate impulses. The world only began to take notice of anthroposophy when we put our intentions into practice by building the Goetheanum, for which the foundation stone was laid in 1913. The Goetheanum made anthroposophy visible to the world. People could now see something they did not understand and that is how the world began to take notice of anthroposophy.

Although we were caught up in old habits even during the war, there was also gradual progress. Scientists who had originally joined the anthroposophical movement out of a profound inner need of soul found that anthroposophy could meet those needs. They also found that the sciences today had reached a dead end.

This dead end is precisely where the true need for knowledge starts. You only need to open your eyes to the state of the sciences today: young students are presented with a body of knowledge that has specific characteristics. Nothing is ever said of the qualities of this knowledge that young people find today not only in universities but already in schools. It is a knowledge permeated with materialistic thinking. A lot is said today about materialism having run its course and science returning to the spirit, but these are only empty words, mere illusion. People speak of the spirit without having a concept of it.

Young people are presented with a body of materialistically conceived knowledge; it is poured out on them without giving them any orientation. All they have as orientation is that they will have to pass exams. That gives them some kind of grounding, but on the whole, they hardly know what to do with the whole breadth of scientific life. It is poured out on them and they are left feeling like someone who is surprised by heavy rain. They get soaked through and through, or in actual fact hardened, by this downpour. It would be wrong to say that what is offered to them is worthless. It is not; it is even highly valuable at times, but the students know nothing of this value because of the way knowledge is conveyed to them. Today's knowledge may be ever so valuable but it will not reach the consciousness of those who are expected to absorb it.

May I refer you in all modesty to the part of my autobiography that has been published: you will find a remarkable phenomenon there. I don't describe there *how* I learned. What was presented to me at school, remained external in a way. What I gained from school, I gained through individual personalities who made a certain impression on me.

In the recent [weekly magazine] *Das Goetheanum* I called attention to how I was taught chemistry in the middle school. Chemistry is something admirable today but the way it is presented as a science is not coherent. Knowledge pours over you like rain.

My middle school chemistry teacher was a brilliant chemist. He spoke very little. He carried out experiments in front of us, continually, only saying a few words here or there to link one experiment to the next. This would go on for weeks until it was time for grades. I left out some more intimate details in my account, but the students knew that when it was time for grades, old Gilm would ask them questions. He never asked before, just did his experiments in front of us for weeks. One of us summoned the courage to go to him and ask, 'Dr Gilm, will there be an experiment or an examination next?' He replied, 'Well, there will an exam.' Then he tested us thoroughly for two or three lessons. It was an excellent method but it did not really help us to enter into the subject.

This chemistry teacher, Hugo von Gilm, was the brother of a Tyrolean poet called Herman von Gilm. Someone who is sensitive to such things would learn more chemistry from looking into the eyes of Hugo von Gilm than from hours of systematic tuition, although we gained much from that, too. He had very special eyes. The way they looked into the world made you realize that he took in very deeply what he perceived in nature. His eyes would take it in and radiate it out again. It lived in him, which is why we boys always felt that he had a different relationship to his science than all other teachers. We would address the other teachers as 'Professor', but him, although he was a professor, too, we would call 'Doctor' because we sensed that he related differently to his science than others. It was his personality! From other examples I mention in the book you can also see that it was always about personality. Personalities always had something stimulating for me. This is how I was able to sleep through school but found out the interesting things myself.

In the second half of the nineteenth century and in the twentieth century one could not learn anything unless one actively searched for knowledge. Learning then happened on the side, and I must say it almost surprises me that I was a good student given that we were given grades according to what we learned at school. I didn't really learn anything there. It is surprising that I did well in all subjects.

I think it is essential that we realize how damaging the transmission of knowledge is today. Quite a few scientists who have joined the Anthroposophical Society certainly recognize that. They realize that the sciences have come to a dead end, to a point where the soul wants to transform what science has to offer into true knowledge. Dear friends, there is no human knowledge that is uninteresting if it is taught and received in the right way. And yet, how often are pupils and students bored by their lessons today! This has induced a few scientists to join the Anthroposophical Society, seeking to enliven the individual sciences through anthroposophy.

Now something happened that really upset people. It was not only the Goetheanum that upset them but also the anthroposophical approach to science. Anthroposophy impacted on things in a way that was not well received.

It is insight that is missing. What I have said before in an anthroposophical meeting is true: there are always enemies at anthroposophical conferences and hostility is closely connected with naivety. We find that naivety is widespread among our members. One may think it is easy to convince priests, professors or physicians, but it is not. Most people today cannot be convinced either intellectually or emotionally. What counts for them is having a certain status in life. They may not be conscious of this but they cannot get away from it. One needs to know these things. People who have a certain status in life today cannot simply break away from it. This is how opposition to anthroposophy arises, stirred of course by dishonest people. Hardly a week passes without some kind of pamphlet or book being published against anthroposophy.

There is no need to remind you of the consequences of the threefolding movement in Germany. I can restrict myself to qualitative aspects. As a result of all these things the old peace that prevailed before the world took notice of anthroposophy ceased. Now we need to defend and foster anthroposophy as it is attacked and vilified from all sides. This led to the question which has lived so strongly here in the last days of November and in early December among those who were prepared to take on the

Leadership of the anthroposophical movement. The question was how one can do more anthroposophy in the future. For anthroposophy has always been pursued, and can only be pursued, in a peaceful environment. Because we no longer have that, we need to find ways of bringing anthroposophy to the world without it being attacked and vilified because of the approach it takes. Ways must be found to realize anthroposophy in the way it was intended from the very beginning.

This is what brought a particular quality to the Christmas Conference, which now lies in the past. We must not treat the Christmas Conference as we do so many other things in the Anthroposophical Society. Something new needs to radiate out from this Christmas Conference; something new that is at the same time an extension of what went before. The Society will therefore include what I have referred to in the second Newsletter as 'the School of Spiritual Science'.

Mistakes have been made regarding the School of Spiritual Science when the thread of true anthroposophical life was severed. When we discussed the Goetheanum, which has been taken from us, I already mentioned how little the academic courses had been in keeping with the Goetheanum's artistic style. They were the exact opposite. This was because people tried to bring into the Goetheanum what lives in the universities. But that is not needed. It would only be needed if we sought some kind of official recognition for our School. What we need more than anything is a place that provides what cannot be found anywhere else: guidance towards the spiritual world. Precisely that will become the content of the School of Spiritual Science.

All schools that lead to the spirit started with an exoteric circle that then progressed towards esoteric knowledge. The Leadership of the Anthroposophical Society really wants to embrace what is naturally required for spirit knowledge. In the second article on the School of Spiritual Science, which is to be continued, I started describing our future intentions. We will have the Anthroposophical Society, which can be joined under the conditions set out in the Statutes and discussed at the Christmas Conference. People will remain in the Anthroposophical Society for a while; they may even find they are fully satisfied with the spirit knowledge they can acquire there. If you read carefully what it says in the second Newsletter you will agree that it is only right that those who join the General Anthroposophical Society learn about spirit knowledge there for that is the basis of any path into the spiritual world.

There must of course first be people who conduct spiritual research and pass on the knowledge gained. However, a special karma is required for someone to approach spiritual vision without having first learned about the ideas arising from spiritual research. Generally, people are quite able to understand the spiritual ideas and insights brought to them without relying on authority. Members of the Anthroposophical Society should therefore first study anthroposophy and experience all the implications these studies will have on the different aspects of their life. Only then should they embark on an esoteric path. The three classes of the School of Spiritual Science, which will now be developed out of the general Society, will offer esoteric content organized in Sections as described during the Christmas Conference.

Today, we have many friends in the Anthroposophical Society who have been members for a long time. Anyone joining today would be advised to remain in the Anthroposophical Society for two years before applying for admission to the First Class of the School of Spiritual Science. This condition can naturally not apply to members who are what would today commonly be termed 'old hands' at anthroposophy.

The First Class will therefore be established at once, and we have announced that people can now apply for membership. I have in fact already received many applications. We will start the First Class soon and older members will be admitted to it. However, we will not be pedantic about this. Mature younger members who are deeply committed to anthroposophy will also be able to join the First Class. It will always be more about inner than outer aspects.

Some external changes will be necessary first. I realized some time ago that three lectures a week are excessive, given the way they have been received, particularly more recently. There have been too many lectures. Don't be upset when I say this. I will now start—things will change step by step—to speak for the Anthroposophical Society on Saturdays and Sundays, and on Fridays I will speak for the First Class of the School of Spiritual Science.

We shall have general membership cards for the Anthroposophical Society in future and will introduce separate membership cards for the First Class. On Fridays the members of the First Class of the School of Spiritual Science will gather here, on Saturdays and Sundays it will be all members of the Anthroposophical Society. I expect that First Class members will also be here on Saturdays and Sundays because I would like to arrange things so that everyone can see here in Dornach that the Christmas Conference is taking effect.

From the first lecture I gave in Dornach many years ago about the acanthus leaf we have gradually moved forward and more and more esoteric truths have been heard here. That is too much, though, for new members. We need to demonstrate here in Dornach not only what can be achieved in the Anthroposophical Society but also how this is done. We can do this best if I initially continue in the First Class on Fridays from what we did up to the lecture last Sunday, speaking also about inner developments; in brief, fostering the esoteric side. That will be on Fridays. On Saturdays and Sundays, I will present an introduction to anthroposophy. I will naturally not read or repeat what can be found in my books *Theosophy* and *How to Know Higher Worlds* but try nonetheless to present the foundations of anthroposophy. I expect that the will to participate in the anthroposophical life will not be restricted to people saying here in Dornach: 'We are only going to attend on Fridays for we already know everything else.' Rather, I hope that the members of the First Class will show more interest in the general lectures for they will hear much there that has previously been neglected. Members will experience here in future how anthroposophy can come to life from its very foundations. They will also be able to receive the esoteric content of the First Class if they have applied for membership and this has been granted.

It is important that this constitution of the Anthroposophical Society will be understood. I hope to find a way of working by Sunday so that I will be able to start on Friday of next week with what I propose for the three evenings. Tomorrow I will start with my presentation of the foundations of anthroposophy.

Here in Dornach in particular, it will be possible to receive impulses arising from the Christmas Conference. Based on these explanations people will willingly embrace the 'more anthroposophy' approach.

Anthroposophy cannot be theory only, nor can it be entirely without it. We live at a time when anthroposophy could become a burning question for many people on earth if the Anthroposophical Society only succeeded in kindling the necessary interest through its mode of working.

Let me give you an example of what I mean by this: Henry Ford has published the story of his life, a delightful and very impressive work. The way this 'king of automobiles' describes his life's yearnings, both spiritual and material, makes me imagine someone with urgent spiritual needs standing before a door. What he longs for is urgent and justified but he does not have the voice to express it. He wants to shout it out into the world but that doesn't seem loud enough and so he starts knocking and hammering on the door to make himself heard.

Reading Ford's book, I almost feel as if *I* were standing at that door. And yet it is delightful. You feel bruised inwardly but you love the bruises because it is all so incredibly reasonable. Behind the door is anthroposophy which, however, has not yet been developed sufficiently to grant access to those who stand outside knocking at the door. There is no way in. We need something entirely different.

Ford is representative of something. Many people today have the same experience as he has, although his is on a much grander scale. The future needs more than awareness of what it means to be a good student of anthroposophy. Dear friends, I am not saying anything against students of anthroposophy; their aspirations are entirely reasonable. They have found anthroposophy. They had the best time while there was peace and while anthroposophy was growing. There is nothing wrong with wanting to learn. That is one thing. It is even true that anthroposophy needs to be fostered much more deeply in future than it has been after 1918, when people tried to bring all kinds of academic and other affectations into the anthroposophical movement. It has always been necessary to represent anthroposophy in the world. This has been attempted but it requires an entirely different style. It was this that induced me to take on the presidency: it will enable me to show the world how I would like anthroposophy to be presented by the Society. When in 1912/1913—with good intentions at the time—I stepped down [as president] aiming to restrict my activities to teaching, this turned out to be impossible, because my real intentions were permanently blunted by the Society. After 1918 especially, these impulses lost their momentum.

The special arrangements I have just described for Dornach—they are only a beginning and will be developed further—will show how anthroposophy is to be represented, how it is to be presented to the world. That is also the best way of carrying it into the members' hearts. Of the two sides, the one that thrived during the peaceful period will thrive even more. And we will find that by cultivating this in the right way—as intended by the Leadership—we will also be able to say to those who are hammering on the door: 'Behind the door is anthroposophy.' The way things are now, people can hammer all they like, the door remains closed! If ways could only be found for anthroposophy to open the door from within! But that would presuppose that people of our time like Ford, with the knowledge they have today, can say: 'I wrote that today's science is oriented to the past, but we cannot live in the past only; there must be a future life. We cannot just absorb knowledge; we also need something that is alive. I have now written this down (read the second last chapter, for example, in Ford's intriguing book) and now I know that something is missing, and that something is anthroposophy.' There is a possibility that people would say something like that if we knew how to take the intentions of the Christmas Conference seriously, if the content of the Christmas Conference did not fade away but grow.

This is what I wanted to say today, dear friends, as an introduction to how we will work here in Dornach in the future. Tomorrow I will begin to look at the Anthroposophical Society as it should be thought of as the home of anthroposophy.

I would like to call your attention to a eurythmy performance to be presented here on Sunday at five. The corresponding lectures will be on Saturday and Sunday at eight.

[*Translated by Margot M. Saar*]

Newsletter, 20 January 1924

I.

If the intentions of the Christmas Conference are to be achieved, the Anthroposophical Society will, in the future, have to bring to fulfilment the esoteric striving of its members whenever possible. In striving for this fulfilment, three classes of a School will be integrated into the General Society.

It is in the nature of spirit knowledge that it first brings to human beings results found by individuals who know the paths to spiritual perception. It is a prejudice to think that such results can be endorsed only by those who are themselves able to find them. This prejudice then gives rise to another: that people who offer their own endorsement are surrendering themselves to a blind faith in authority. When this prejudice is asserted, a society like the Anthroposophical Society stands accused of having a membership made up of people who mindlessly worship its leading personalities.

Just as one need not be a painter in order to sense the beauty in a picture, one need not be a spiritual researcher in order to understand the wide scope of what the spiritual researcher has to say. By means of the capacities present in them, these researchers approach the worlds in which spiritual beings live and spiritual events take place. They observe these spiritual beings and events, and also observe how the beings and events of the physical world arise out of what is spiritual.

They have the further task of shaping certain areas of their perceptions into ideas that do not depend on special capacities but are, instead, accessible to ordinary consciousness. Anyyone who brings these ideas to life in their soul finds them intrinsically justifiable. Such ideas cannot be formed out of mere capacities for thought; they can be created only when spiritual perceptions are re-cast in ideas. However, once they exist by means of the spiritual researcher's efforts, every person is able to internalize them and find their inherent justification. It is not necessary to accept them based on mere blind faith. If some believe that what the spiritual researcher advances in the form of ideas is not in and of itself understandable, this is only a result of their having lost the way to such an understanding. Such individuals have grown accustomed to accepting as demonstrable only what is supported by sensory observation; they have no appreciation for the fact that ideas themselves can offer evidence for one another. They are like someone who knows that all heavy objects are supported by the earth and who therefore believes that the earth itself must also be supported by something in space.

An individual must be especially predestined to achieve direct perception in the spirit before first acquiring the results of such perception in the form of ideas. For all others, the necessary first step for attaining their own spiritual perception is to understand the idea-content of that realm of the spiritual world that can be conveyed in the form of ideas.

Yet another prejudice is the belief that people are deluding themselves about perceiving a spiritual world after having an image of that world suggested to them in the form of an idea. It makes little sense to speak about delusion when we see a person we have only heard about before. It makes just as little sense to speak about suggestion when a person perceives the effect of the emerging spiritual world with all its characteristics of reality after having first understood it in the form of ideas.

In general, then, it will have to be necessary to become acquainted with the spiritual world first in the form of ideas. Spiritual science will be cultivated in this way in the General Anthroposophical Society.

There will be those who want presentations about the spiritual world that ascend from the ideas to forms of expression borrowed from the spiritual world itself. And there will also be people who want to become acquainted with paths into the spiritual world so that they may traverse them with their own souls.

The three classes of the School will be there for such people. And in these classes, the work will ascend to ever-higher degrees of esotericism. The School will guide its participants up into realms of the spiritual world that cannot be revealed in the form of ideas. For these realms, ways must be found to express imaginations, inspirations, and intuitions.

Aspects of artistic, pedagogical, and ethical life—among others—can then be brought into realms where they may receive illumination and creative impulses from the esoteric.

The organization of the 'School' and its structuring into Sections will be discussed in the next edition of the Newsletter.

[*Translated by Marguerite Miller and Douglas Miller*]

Newsletter, 27 January 1924

II.

We are unable to found branch institutions of the Goetheanum everywhere souls yearn for anthroposophy—for we are a poor Society.

To the extent we continue sharing in writing what takes place at the Goetheanum, we will be able to make it possible for people who live far away from the Goetheanum to take part in its work. How this written exchange will take place has yet to be discussed. Such exchanges also enable those who cannot spend an extended time at the Goetheanum to participate in the classes there. Whenever possible, this exchange will be assisted by visits to various places from leaders at the Goetheanum or their close associates.

If the esoteric life of the School is to thrive and flourish, however, all this must be held together by the genuine spirit of anthroposophy.

The Leadership of the Goetheanum must endeavour to avoid insulating itself in any way from the spiritual life of the present time. Instead, it must be fully engaged in seeking out what is revealed through this spiritual life for the true further development of humanity.

Sections will therefore be guided by individuals who take on the administration of their Sections; some Sections are already possible and will blossom—we hope—through increased activity.

The General Anthroposophical Section will occupy a place in the centre; the Pedagogical Section will be provisionally situated in it. I myself will be responsible for the leadership of that Section. A Medical Section will see to it that anthroposophy can fructify medical healing. Its leadership will be in the hands of Dr Ita Wegman. From ancient times, medicine has had an intimate spiritual relationship with the central tasks of human knowledge. Anthroposophy should show its vitality by re-establishing this connection. Dr Wegman's Clinical-Therapeutic Institute has created a model for this endeavour and its practical implications.

Anthroposophy must have artistic life near to its heart. Through the cultivation of eurythmy during the past several years, through the arts of declamation and recitation, we have a budding, new artistic life. The element of musicality is closely connected with this. The cultivation of this life will occur in one particular Section. Mrs Marie Steiner has connected her work to this artistic life with great devotion. Based on the history of the Anthroposophical Society itself, she is named to the leadership of this Section.

The visual arts came to light during the Goetheanum's construction. A style unfolded in the pivotal work developed on this ground—a style that by its very nature must find many opponents, even today. Of course, at the present time this style can only give imperfect expression to what it intends. But it will be better understood as people come closer to anthroposophy in general. Miss E. Maryon has helped me in the development of this style in a way that calls for her to be the leader of the Sculptural Arts Section.

There was once a concept known as the *Schöne Wissenschaften*—the 'beautiful sciences'. They built a bridge between actual science and the activity of creative human imagination. The view of 'science' developed more recently has pushed the 'beautiful sciences' completely into the background. I will discuss the 'beautiful sciences' in a forthcoming issue of *Das Goetheanum*. We in the Anthroposophical Society are fortunate to have in our midst a splendid representative of the 'beautiful sciences': Albert Steffen. For this reason, he is called not only to be the leader of the Section for the Literary Arts and Humanities but also to re-enliven this branch of human creativity that has been pushed off into a corner—to the grave detriment of civilization.

Furthermore, circumstances allow us to establish Sections based on our work with certain individuals. Thus a Section for mathematical and astronomical considerations will be led by Dr L. Vreede; and a Natural Science Section will be led by Dr Guenther Wachsmuth. The realm of astronomy is particularly important to anthroposophy; and the Natural Science Section should demonstrate how a genuine knowledge of nature does not contradict anthroposophy but is in full accord with it. With the publication of his forthcoming book, Dr G. Wachsmuth shows himself to be the right person to lead this Section.

[*Translated by Marguerite and Douglas Miller*]

The School of Spiritual Science within the Constitution of the Anthroposophical Society—Its Organization in Sections

Lecture by Rudolf Steiner on 30 January 1924

We must now gradually arrive at the point of establishing here in Dornach something like a model of what must exist in the Anthroposophical Society from now on. However, this can only take place if here in Dornach there is also a genuine, thoroughgoing, and overarching understanding of what the arrangement of the Society and its general constitution are intended to be in the future.

Based on the letters I have received as applications for the class, I have seen that such a general understanding does not yet exist. Therefore, before we establish what is to be created, I will have to speak more here about what has to happen, and I will therefore offer the next three lectures—on Friday, Saturday, and Sunday—as general lectures for all members of the Anthroposophical Society. The arrangement of the lectures for the various classes will begin next week when it will be completely clear who will be involved in the First Class, the one that will be established initially.

For example, some elements prominent in certain letters need to disappear. There were letters that simply requested permission to attend not only the lectures on Saturday and Sunday, but also the Friday lectures. Now, you see, this suggests that what is meant by a structuring of the Society as such and the classes to be established in it has not yet been sufficiently understood. And today I would like to say a few words about that.

There is no significance attached to the day when lectures will be offered to members of the First Class in the future. It might even be that we schedule lectures for the General Society on Friday and Saturday, and lectures for members of the First Class on Sunday. This means that the matter cannot be taken so superficially. An indication of the fact that it cannot be taken so superficially is the strict way these things are expressed in the Statutes. The main point is to realize what the Anthroposophical Society is to become.

Everyone who hears about the Anthroposophical Society should be able to recognize right away that it has nothing to do with some sort of secretiveness; that it is a completely public Society like other societies. I would have preferred that this had been understood right from the moment when the Anthroposophical Society was first established in 1912, 1913. Everything would have been much easier than it is now. As an integral part of the arrangements at that time, I established that I myself would stand apart from the actual administration of the Anthroposophical Society; I wanted nothing more than to be the person who provides the store of knowledge or the impulses that were to flow into the Anthroposophical Society. This might have made it possible for the Anthroposophical Society to work easily in the world in terms of the impression given by anthroposophy generally—because the individual providing the impulses and the Society's leadership were not united in a single person.

This did not happen and that is why it has now become necessary for me to provide the impulses and also take on leadership of the Society, something I wished to avoid earlier.

This was really a very difficult decision. Everything needed to change fundamentally and it will be quite difficult now to make these changes—to make basic changes in this or that element—in view of many practices that have become ingrained over the years.

The Anthroposophical Society must really come to recognize fully two aspects of its situation. The first is that it needs to be conscious that it exists for all human beings in the world who seek in their soul the paths to what is spiritual. It is a completely public Society in this respect—a Society that must be quite independent outwardly. Therefore, within the Anthroposophical Society we should not be at all narrow-minded when admitting members.

If this is sufficiently recognized, the presence of this or that person who is perhaps not very well suited to anthroposophical things need not present a difficulty for the Anthroposophical Society. Only when the Anthroposophical Society is made responsible for every single individual in it will difficulties naturally arise. The Anthroposophical Society as such should have no limits placed on its potential for giving everyone what they are seeking in the way indicated.

But secondly, the Anthroposophical Society should be clear about the fact that it was not formed out of some sort of unidentifiable or vague intention. It could even have been quite clear about that in 1912, 1913, because a large part of its teachings were already present at that time, and certain impulses also existed then that were intended to realize here in the physical world what the spiritual world wills to tell us in the present time. We might well imagine that the Anthroposophical Society was not oriented toward abstract principles at that time, saying you should make this or that your ideal. Even then it was founded on what is in fact present, what exists, what had been achieved over a long period. And the cultivation of this achievement with all its implications for artistic, religious, and social life—in brief, in all branches of human life, and the working out these implications—these are the on-going responsibilities of the Anthroposophical Society.

Now when this is understood in the right way, the Anthroposophical Society becomes different from every other society in the world today. They are not founded on anything that actually exists but on all manner of human intentions instead. That is why the Statutes emphasize so strongly that the Anthroposophical Society consists of those individuals who see the spiritual life that flows from the Goetheanum as justified. There is nothing in them about keeping to this or that principle, but everything is based on what presently exists among human beings, or at least can exist among human beings.

This is what is so important. And we might even say: If the Anthroposophical Society wants to develop in itself a consciousness of the times, it cannot do so without taking into account what I have just said. For our time, our present time, is actually—please take this phrase quite seriously—the time for great decisions. Much is being decided in the present time for humanity, enormous things. Of course, this current epoch will last for a long time, but much—immeasurably much—is presently being decided for humanity. Many people are just not aware of the significance of the present time as one of great decisions. And it is especially important that a strong consciousness of these decisions be developed in the Anthroposophical Society. So from one aspect, we must say that the Anthroposophical Society should not, for example, establish a principle like this: I am choosing people I trust and they can then decide who they will or will not accept according to their own sympathies and antipathies. This has already happened to a fairly large extent and that is why it has gradually come to a point where so many people who want to join feel repelled by the Anthroposophical Society. Again and again you hear the statement: 'Anthroposophy is fine but anthroposophists are intolerable.' Almost every day we meet the practical consequences of this.

It would be extremely difficult for the Anthroposophical Society to tend to what must be done for the cultivation of anthroposophy if the Society did not demonstrate an understanding for the greatest possible open-mindedness as well as the greatest possible enthusiasm. Anthroposophy itself cannot abide narrow-mindedness and apathy.

Everywhere today you can see how those human relationships that have spiritual substance in them are working energetically to care for the relationships they have achieved by means of this spiritual substance. Today we see how everywhere these human groups—large groups of human beings around the world—are beginning to work in the most active way because this is the time of great decisions in human hearts.

The Anthroposophical Society can actually become something that has a voice in the present time if the intentions I just indicated are taken up by its members.

It is especially important that there be more and more clarity about how to conceive of the relationship between an individual member and the Anthroposophical Society itself. You see, what we might call the teachings or the impulses of the Anthroposophical Society can be understood by anyone who simply wants to use their common sense. It is not at all the case that someone needs something like an initiation, etc., for insight, for an understanding of what stands before the world as anthroposophy. What stands before the world as anthroposophy can be understood if only someone is unprejudiced enough! To be sure, this lack of prejudice is difficult in our time because humanity has almost completely lost its connection with the spiritual world. And wherever we look today we meet judgements like the one I will now cite. We hear: 'Well, certainly, there is a spiritual world but the spiritual world is simply a mystery. Human understanding is not suited for reaching any kind of insight about the spiritual world.' And so it is actually seen as a hallmark for a real perception of the spiritual world that this spiritual world should appear as something mysterious. Something that cannot be known, something we can only have a vague sense for, something we should only feel at best, and so forth—that is what is seen as the true spiritual element. And it is unpleasant for people to admit that what is spiritual should actually be understood. Most people do not have the courage for it. Most people find it quite comfortable to say: 'The spiritual is something we must vaguely sense, something we cannot understand, something secret.' Now, the whole of spiritual science depends on unveiling the secret so that the mystery really appears before the world.

It might be said that the only large institution—although this is not always rightly understood even by those who belong to this institution—the only large institution that actually sets out to place this mystery before the world, to reveal it, is the Catholic Church. The Catholic Church—when it is rightly understood—has no way to understand the statement: 'What is contained in the spiritual world cannot be expressed in ideas, in concepts.' For it lies in the whole nature of the Catholic Church to express in concepts what is mysterious—i.e., what at first seems veiled from the sensory world. The whole mood I characterized just now really did not arise until the last few centuries. But, this mood needs to disappear again today. We must understand once again that the task of humanity is to unveil for itself what is mysterious.

During the 1880s, when I met many of those who were members of the Theosophical Society in Vienna—some belonging to the most intimate circles of the Theosophical Society—the phrase 'profoundly deep' was heard again and again. The simplest statements were often cited by these people, the simplest things, but it was noted that human beings could not understand these very simple things because they were 'profoundly deep'. And if you asked how they understood the matter, they would reply that it was impossible to say because it was 'profoundly deep'. Well then, the Anthroposophical Society should not work by talking around the mystery and just noting that it is mysterious. The Anthroposophical Society should be concerned that everyone in it—otherwise there is no reason for joining it—is really familiar with what anthroposophy can offer about the spiritual world. Each member should begin by making an effort to understand what the Society itself can offer. This is really not asking too much. As I have noted before, pedantry has no authority here. It will not be a matter of following the guidelines I am giving here in some pedantic way or unconditionally. There must always be exceptions and numerous exceptions will be necessary in one way or another. But two years are really needed to orient oneself inwardly about what the Anthroposophical Society is offering now that its teaching and impulses have been worked out over the years. Anyone who has not been in the Anthroposophical Society for two years is not well-advised to enter a class immediately. It is best for them not to think of that at all, but to begin by thinking about really cultivating what is there as anthroposophy—and there is indeed enough anthroposophy available.

And here I come right to what is important about the Anthroposophical Society. In the third section of what I addressed to the members I briefly pointed to this as the important thing about the Society.

If we look at these things from the outside, we can say: what anthroposophy offers is found in books, in public lectures; I can learn about this for myself—in fact, anyone can—and basically there can be no objection to someone saying this. And there is no harm—quite the opposite, it will be very good—if as many people as possible in the world maintain this position and say: I do not need a society; I am engaged with what is offered in the literature or otherwise becomes public out of anthroposophy—after all, the Anthroposophical Society exists to bring life to anthroposophy. And here, something appears that also justifies the Society even though anthroposophy is already available.

Anthroposophy is meant to live among human beings. And the point is: if anthroposophy lives among human beings, we really need to take into account what it means to pursue a common spiritual goal with others. It means very much.

People might attend a branch meeting of the Anthroposophical Society. Something can be said there in a more or less skilled manner, something those attending have long known because they read it somewhere. In any case, there is something not right with the Society if they leave with the impression: 'I did not need to go because I already knew what was being presented.' It must be possible in the context of the Anthroposophical Society for judgements to be based on perceptions of the real situation.

When people eat, they normally do not say: 'I did not need to eat chicken now because I already know how chicken tastes. I know what chicken is like in my mouth, on my tongue. Why do I need to eat chicken since I am already quite familiar with its effect on me?' That is nonsense—absurd, is it not?

And likewise, it should not be possible for this judgement to arise: 'I don't need to attend the anthroposophical members' meeting because I already know what is being offered there.' But if this to be felt in the right way, one should not attend meetings of the Society or its branches simply in order to find out what might be said there or even debated there. One should attend because human beings are there. One must attend for the sake of the human beings.

And this is what must be thoroughly understood: one does not enter the Anthroposophical Society simply to be instructed but rather to be together with those human beings who are in the Anthroposophical Society or its various branches. Whether the Anthroposophical Society will flourish or not depends upon whether there is a feeling for the life of anthroposophy within human souls, not only in one's own soul but in human souls. Otherwise it will always be the case that people who enter the Anthroposophical Society do so to learn something. But if they want to find human beings they go instead to where human beings really meet one another: to five o'clock teas, or other things I will not mention here. I think the human being needs human beings. Within the Anthroposophical Society it cannot reach the point that people attend for reasons other than the human beings there. And care must be taken that we enter the Anthroposophical Society for the sake of the human beings in whom anthroposophy lives. Thus an entirely new element enters the life of anthroposophy within the Society, an element that must be there. A purely human factor enters. These are things for which there is truly an urgent longing in our time.

You know that during the Christmas Conference we asked certain individuals to write about their experiences of modern spiritual life out in the world; that they write to Mr Steffen, the editor of the *Newsletter* and of *Das Goetheanum*, about their experiences of spiritual life within the Society and also outside the Society. And I discussed the importance of this in the last Newsletter.

As a result of this effort, all sorts of interesting things we already knew have re-emerged. For example: the religious community for Christian renewal—you know that they received their impulses from anthroposophy; they work as a self-sufficient community but received their impulses from anthroposophical content—this community very recently held a meeting in Kassel. This meeting in Kassel had a unique quality—something very characteristic of the present. It consisted of participants who were either rather young or were already more advanced in years. The reporter says that most of the people there were in their early twenties, and then there were people from the age of 35 or 38 and upwards. But the years in between—the humanity between, in their twenties and thirties—were missing from this gathering. This is quite characteristic. It is especially meaningful—if you look with open eyes, you see this everywhere—that in all the significant issues and decisions in the world during recent years, the people who were absent were the ones who were most important, those between the ages of 20, or 22 and 38 etc. I am not saying that the others are not important; but the important thing is that these other people be present, too. Then the younger people and the older people can really do something. But if those in precisely this important age group are missing—and you can find the importance of this time of life in many anthroposophical indications—then difficulties arise.

Nevertheless, all sorts of things resulted from this meeting in Kassel. The organization was handled entirely by The Christian Community. To begin with, smaller circles of people were formed and then guided to ascend to the higher truths, guided towards what The Christian Community has to say from an independent religious point of view. Something else was added by The Christian Community: the ritual act. The week passed in this way, from Wednesday to Sunday, I think; and on Sunday the ritual act was added. This was followed by two or three days for discussion during which people could speak with one another. It became evident how these people, based on a real, pressing need of the human heart in the present time, ascended with all their soul through these days to the ritual act, and how all of them later inquired: 'Isn't there something more to this? All this can only be preparation. There has to be something more.'

It turned out that what people were longing for is anthroposophy. And there will likely be fine results from this youth conference in Kassel; for example, others will now think about pedagogical renewal, just as The Christian Community has thought about religious renewal. If pedagogical renewal is approached with all this energy, something can really happen.

I cite this instance because it shows that, in truth, anthroposophy does not stem from some sort of selfish intention but rather from something for which the modern human soul longs. And if the human soul is prepared through the realm of feelings then, of necessity, it arrives not only at the point where the mystery is no longer left blurry and indistinct but at a point where the soul actually takes hold of the unveiled mystery through anthroposophy. The Anthroposophical Society must no longer be an obstacle to this activity of carrying into the world what the world is longing for, what countless hearts, countless souls are longing for. And this is the reason for establishing the Anthroposophical Society as a fully public Society during the Christmas Conference.

But everything we are setting out to establish must be comprehensible at the very moment it exists, the moment it arises—in part it must be comprehensible based on reason, in part based on feeling. After all, our anthroposophy—as well as its pedagogical element—can be comprehended by the unprejudiced human being. Nothing more is necessary than an application of healthy human understanding as long as this healthy human understanding is not constrained by the prejudices that exist in the present time. Thus we can say: The Anthroposophical Society must be fully based on comprehension, on nothing other than comprehension. And, of course, anyone who is simply a member of the Anthroposophical Society cannot be required to become a carrier or active worker in anthroposophy. It is completely justified for the individual member merely to seek out anthroposophy and also anthroposophical people within the Society. And there is really no immediate expectation that a member of the Anthroposophical Society should contribute to its dissemination.

What I said in one instalment of my letters to the members must remain true: the Anthroposophical cause must not proselytize in the usual sense of the word; any such proselytizing is wrong—it is not necessary to proselytize for anthroposophy; it is only necessary to give people what they are yearning for anyway, so long as ways are found that allow people to express what they long for. They are least likely to express this longing if we act like arrogant pedants and tell them: 'I have arrived at this conviction and you must believe it—otherwise you are a nitwit, and anyone who does not believe what I believe is a nitwit.' It is very important that we acquire the attitude that we have no right to give people something other than what they yearn for, or that we have a right to think of ourselves as superior to the people to whom we want to bring something. We must rid ourselves of the habit of acting in the usual pedantic or proselytizing manner. We really need to follow through with the thought that a genuine comprehension must serve as the basic element of life in the Anthroposophical Society.

But the Anthroposophical Society must also be administered, its body of knowledge must be administered, and people are required for that. And the administration of the body of knowledge has now to be thought of in the context of the Christmas Conference. Those who carry this administration must now also be individuals who turn to the classes in cooperation with the designated Executive Council and the Leadership at the Goetheanum. Because understanding anthroposophy does not call on an element of trust. But what is needed to administer anthroposophy, of course, is complete trust in the person who works within its administration. Thus the organization of the classes is where the atmosphere of trust begins; it is here that we really must build on trust. And I have said for as long as there has been an Anthroposophical Society: There is no contradiction in asserting that anthroposophy should not be taken on authority nor on trust but be based on comprehension. At the same time, the administration of the anthroposophical cause can only be built on trust.

In regard to people who undertake something, who have something for which they are responsible, who have something to cultivate, it is necessary that human trust prevail. Within the class this question of trust must actually be taken as seriously as open- mindedness is in regard to the Anthroposophical Society.

It is therefore necessary for people who wish to become members of the classes to ask themselves whether they really want from the outset to stand for the anthroposophical cause before the world and represent it with all their courage and in every way.

In fact, it is true that the esoteric deepening you can read about in my book *Knowledge of Higher Worlds and Its Attainment*—deepening so often spoken of—will now begin to take place through the three classes.

This cannot happen if the members of these classes do not feel themselves to be true representatives of the anthroposophical cause, if they do not ask themselves whether they are really ready to take it upon themselves to represent the anthroposophical cause before the world in some way. Of course, not everyone can represent it in its totality—that is not needed, nor is it even useful. But a member can represent it in a particular area. However, to do so they must truly stand completely in the realm of trust—I am not now speaking of the realm of trust necessary for anthroposophy—but in that realm of trust required for the administration of the anthroposophical cause. And here a particular practice has to stop, something so prevalent in earlier times within the Anthroposophical Society—again, I have mentioned this in the third instalment of my letters to the members that will appear this week—in that third instalment I call it 'playing with esotericism'. This can be understood as playing with esotericism in its broadest sense. Esotericism is really an extraordinarily serious matter in regard to one's own soul, to the human being, and to our age. That is not to say that seriousness is demonstrated by making a long face, being as sentimental as possible, and acting self-important; instead, an inner seriousness must be present, even one compatible with a good sense of humour. However, as an example, the following attitude must stop: 'I know something but I cannot tell you what it is because you are not yet ready for it.' The strangest feelings are aroused by this. Above all, people who say this are behaving quite self-importantly without even noticing that they are doing so.

Certainly, there are things that must be cultivated by a small circle of people but they should not be dealt with in the self-important way just described. On the other hand, esoteric matters are not the sort of thing to gossip about—to be circulated by gossip as so often happens. These things are very difficult to describe because they are based in certain behaviours. But here and there some people will understand what I mean. This content is not being presented just so that it can be said that certain things were a secret in the Mysteries or that certain incarnations happened. It must be treated with the greatest possible seriousness. It must be treated with a certain insight into the following situation. How easy it is to hear the hackneyed claim: 'Oh, those people are doing something, but esoterically you can't get anywhere with them. On the other hand, we—we who are truly worthy—should practise esotericism among ourselves.' In and of itself, that kind of talk contributes enormously to the destruction of the Anthroposophical Society. First of all, this is mostly nothing more than a disguised cliquish satisfaction, the satisfaction of a need for cliques. And furthermore, when people say these things there is no sense for the extent to which an esoteric element is found in all areas of life. Life itself is quite esoteric. And it is hard to believe how much esotericism is found in a university laboratory—it's just that the professors and adjuncts don't realize it. But it is there nonetheless. The esoteric is not found in scorning something else in order to do as one pleases. It is found by engaging with life and its depths in the most energetic way.

This is what I mean when I say, 'playing with esotericism'. Such 'playing with esotericism' also evaporates quite quickly. A circle may be founded based on a disguised need for cliques but it soon disappears. Some people find it too difficult to engage with the real esotericism of life; they find it comfortable to gossip about esotericism. Indeed, where esotericism is passed around from one person to another—no matter how unctuously this may be done—it is still esoteric gossip. And this is really what contributes enormously to the destruction of the Anthroposophical Society, and even directly to the destruction of the anthroposophical cause. In the future, this question of trust will really have to be taken seriously within the classes, and in the deepest sense.

It will just not do to say: 'I have a right to be accepted into a class if I have been in the Society for two years.' Being accepted into a class means that the leadership of the Anthroposophical Society must work with the individual involved. These leaders cannot be made into slaves. They must not be compelled to work with someone they do not want to work with—perhaps because they have found it impossible to do so. A way must now be found—and this is something worth noting—to have the Christmas Conference taken very seriously. It must be possible for the leadership of the School for Spiritual Science to say to those who cannot come to terms with being representatives of the anthroposophical cause: 'Of course, you are very welcome in the General Anthroposophical Society but, unfortunately, you cannot be a member of the class.' This must be possible in the future. This must be taken with the most profound seriousness.

Of course, these things will never happen based on some sort of sympathy and antipathy; they will not be done with a lack of seriousness. However, they must be thoroughly understood. Basically, if members of the School act in opposition to its leadership, what I just indicated will have to occur. We each have our own wishes, don't we? One person wants this, another wants that. Of course, no member of the Anthroposophical Society can be stopped from having their own wishes. If they were stopped, the Anthroposophical Society would become something quite contrary to what it is intended to be; it would become a sect or a secret society. It must not be that.

Now the classes will in no way have the character of a secret society either. Today, secret societies are not possible; the modern age requires something different. But it must be possible for the leadership to work collaboratively only with people with whom they can work. In the future, those who wish to belong to one of the classes will be required to discuss with the Executive Council any and all initiatives they wish to undertake in the context of anthroposophy. That is the only way for the Executive Council to feel responsible for the whole Anthroposophical

Society. And it wants to feel responsible—and it wants to stand for the anthroposophical cause.

It cannot happen that, in the future, someone comes and says: 'Oh, we are doing things that are none of the Executive Council's business.' Of course, you can do that, but then you cannot belong to the classes. It will be necessary for this principle of harmony in attitude to be just as important in our School as it always was in the Mysteries. Otherwise our entire anthroposophical undertaking will never be able to achieve its goal, for these are simply requirements that comply with the underlying laws of the matter.

Of course, someone can say: 'I want to destroy the anthroposophical cause.' Well, anyone is free to say that. But you cannot expect those who wish to lead this anthroposophical cause to agree that there is no need to fulfil the conditions necessary for it.

Whether it is a matter of founding a group or of doing something else, what is important here is that members of a class in the School for Spiritual Science really undertake these things in harmony with the leadership so that the leadership can, in fact, carry this aspect of anthroposophical work in a centralized way.

Anyone who simply wants to enter the School out of curiosity—perhaps in order to hear something in the classes that is different from what they hear in the Anthroposophical Society—should really consider not taking that step. It was no empty phrase when we said at the Christmas Conference that a new impulse must enter into the life of the Anthroposophical Society. You know, the point is not that something secret is being done with the great body of knowledge in the classes; the point is that people really become representatives of the anthroposophy cause—the higher the class, the more this must be the case. And the anthroposophical cause must be something real, not something that can sail around in never-never-land. It must be something real. And then there must be no more scheming behind the backs of the Executive Council. In the future, the administration of the anthroposophical cause will rest fully in the hands of the School for Spiritual Science.

This School will not be a secret Society either. It will take care to assure that people always know what it is doing, to the greatest possible extent. But, just as in the Anthroposophical Society itself, membership in the School will be based only on what makes sense: that human beings wish to cultivate anthroposophy together with others in the School. By the same token, the School for Spiritual Science will more and more charge its members with the strictest responsibilities. Otherwise it will be unable to endure; furthermore, it will make no sense. For example, one of these responsibilities will be to stop acting in a way that has already become a habit to an unbelievable degree: harshly criticizing those qualified individuals who hold responsible positions in our Anthroposophical Society. It is really easy to criticize; but to accomplish something is infinitely more difficult. When people are comfortable in their daily life—only taking care of the things that directly affect them—it is easy for them to criticize those who spend their days doing what must be done within the Anthroposophical Society. A certain attitude is required, one that gives special consideration to what is really being done in the Anthroposophical Society. The question of what we do not like must be set aside. Currently there is considerable talk about what people think is wrong. But we must pay attention to what is being done, what is really happening. That should come to the consciousness of the Society's members—what is really happening. And although the leadership should in no way lay claim to some false authoritative principle, it is to a certain extent correct that the leadership cannot perform its task if everyone who has no idea how something came to be now starts scolding the leadership from all sides.

These are things that I wanted to draw to your attention today because, for example, I have seen that many participants thought it was just a matter of registering for the Friday lectures so they could hear them along with the Saturday and Sunday lectures. Of course, that would be quite nice. But the School for Spiritual Science should consist of people who whole-heartedly feel themselves to be representatives of the anthroposophical cause. I would therefore ask that this be considered first in any decision to enter the class shortly to be established. And it is in this sense that we will attempt to form the First Class in addition to the Friday, Saturday, and Sunday lectures. The next lectures will still be held for all members of the Anthroposophical Society, and among the lectures to be held next week the First Class will have a part.

The Second Class will not be established for some time.

This is what I wanted to say to you today. I scheduled this hour because I found it necessary after reading the portfolio of letters received up to a certain point in time. It has already become a rather thick portfolio but it will grow even thicker. It will grow into multiple volumes. And reading it taught me that it was necessary to say the things I took the liberty of saying today.

I would like to ask that each person who wishes to be accepted into the School for Spiritual Science indicates to me how long they have already been in the Society—because that must be made clear—and whether they are inclined to become engaged in some way or another with what

I said today about the issue of trust—that is, whether they are willing to take on real responsibilities as members of the class. These things would have to appear in the applications.

It may happen that those friends considering making an application will be asked for more information about themselves beyond what is already in the letter. You see, when people write that they want to hear the Friday lectures, even this is hard to respond to because it is not actually a question of whether they want to hear the Friday lectures—these might well be held on Sunday—but whether they wish to be a member of the School for Spiritual Science. That is the point.

These are matters of concern to the members. The organization into Sections will be a matter for the leadership. And the leadership will work this out so that the departments that need to be represented can, in fact, be represented. But that will happen in every class. And everyone will find their particular needs met through agreement with the leadership of their Section just as they will find their general spiritual needs as human beings are met in the General Section of the Anthroposophical Society. Everyone who belongs to one or another Section will also have to belong to the General Anthroposophical Section, for it must be the basis for everything else.

This, then, is what needs to be taken into consideration.

[*Translated by Marguerite Miller and Douglas Miller*]

Newsletter, 3 February 1924

III.

The organization of the School for Spiritual Science will require that those who wish to take part in its endeavours notify its leadership. To begin with, this will involve the organization of the First Class. The remaining two classes will be added after some time. Participants will only be concerned with the classes of the School. The Sections will be constituted so that in each of the classes the leadership can meet the particular aspirations of the class members. In this sense, a person does not become a member of a Section but of a class. However, someone seeking an esoteric deepening in medicine, for example, will be able to find it offered in a step-by-step fashion because the leadership of the Medical Section arranges for it. This is also true for the various artistic and scientific Sections. How class members attain their individual goals through a specific Section will be determined by agreement with the leader of the whole School [Rudolf Steiner] and with the leaders of the Section. The General Anthroposophical Section will have to be there for all members of the School. Acceptance can therefore not be into a Section but only into a class.

Since the School for Spiritual Science must not be an institution of higher learning in the usual sense, it will not seek to enter into competition with such institutions or substitute for them. However, at the Goetheanum, people will be able to find the esoteric deepening they are unable to find in an ordinary institution of higher learning. They will receive at the Goetheanum precisely what the soul is seeking in its striving for knowledge. This striving for knowledge may be concerned with what is common to all human beings; the General Anthroposophical Section exists for those who have only this generally human need to find paths into the spiritual world. It will form an 'esoteric school' for them. The other Sections will be concerned with indicating paths for those who wish to find a specialized orientation in their lives, for example in the sciences, the arts, etc. Thus the School at the Goetheanum will help striving human beings to find what they are striving for in keeping with their individual life circumstances. The School should not be a purely scientific organization but a purely human one; however, it should also fully meet the esoteric needs of the scientist and the artist.

[*Translated by Marguerite and Douglas Miller*]

Conditions for Admission to the First Class of the School of Spiritual Science

Dornach, 3 February 1924

After his lecture, Dr Steiner spoke to members who had applied to join the First Class:

Today's meeting is of course not asking for any commitment yet. It needs some introspection now on the part of the friends who have stayed here to see if they really want to take on the duties required of a School membership. What has often been cited as another condition for such an association of people as we intend to establish asks for the greatest earnestness. I would say that many groups have not even begun to grasp this earnestness.

We have the General Anthroposophical Society which conveys knowledge of the spirit to people today. You can be a member of this Society if you do not wish to take on any duties. There is no need to go beyond membership in the Anthroposophical Society if you do not wish to take on real, earnest duties.

But we need a group of people who are prepared to move from the exoteric to the esoteric, and that cannot be done without taking on certain duties. Anthroposophy would not exist if there were no one willing to take on such duties. With the First Class that I intend to establish, the relationship between the leadership and the individual members is based on a free contract—a free contract that one nonetheless commits to, so that the leadership does not have to feel bound to do things with members that need doing in the First Class if the members in question are not also committing themselves. It is a contract based on freedom that needs to be taken very seriously. That is the only way to enter into true esotericism. What is most important is for all class members to pronounce their firm wish to be representatives for the cultivation of anthroposophy in the world.

Unlike the Society initiated at Christmas, the former Anthroposophical Society was a kind of administrative body which received anthroposophy with the purpose of providing a framework for it. What we need now is that the institution that is radiating out from Dornach now and presenting itself to the world is seen as esoteric in itself. Members of the First Class accept that the Executive Council formed at Christmas is a body that takes full responsibility for anthroposophy in the world and that everything anthroposophical concerns this Executive Council.

Understanding the full depth of this means understanding that we cannot in future accept certain things that have happened here or there in relation to the anthroposophical life, even after Christmas. People were heard saying things like: 'We are doing something for ourselves that does not concern the Executive Council. Why should we concern ourselves with the Executive Council!' Well, First Class members wishing to do something anthroposophical without the Executive Council will in future find that the Executive Council will do its work without them. I would not say this in the General Anthroposophical Society because it has to do with the free contract that exists between the members of the First Class and the Executive Council.

It is a special form that I am describing that could also be described in different terms. But it is the only way to bring some kind of consistency into the life of the School. It will help to gradually achieve the degree of earnestness in the approach to anthroposophy that is required. We will then have a nucleus of people who will feel responsible for what anthroposophy tries to achieve. It will also be a way of avoiding the forming of cliques, because such cliques have done a lot to harm us in the past. We will furthermore not tolerate members who insist on going their own way. If that is what they need, they can do it within the Anthroposophical Society. For class members it is not an option.

These things need to be considered in all earnestness. They need to be taken seriously in the same way things are taken seriously elsewhere in the world, in contexts that are not anthroposophical. Otherwise, the re-founding of the Society at Christmas would have been meaningless. Members, even in the Society close to Dornach, have developed the habit of saying that they didn't want to burden me by asking all kinds of details. The reason why they didn't ask was because it didn't suit them! As a result a number of matters only came to my attention when they had progressed to a point where different solutions were required from the ones that would have sufficed at an earlier stage. What I am trying to say is that everything concerning the content of anthroposophy must have a common ground.

There will be difficulties, no doubt, and they will be challenging for the small group of Executive Council members, but we will see how things develop and initially take them as they come. We do not want to make the mistake again of consulting the Executive Council for relatively unimportant matters whilst saying with the most important ones: 'We can deal with this ourselves (because we prefer it) and need not trouble the Executive Council with it.' People may get stuck in formalities and ask, 'Where is the freedom here?' Well, they are free not to join!

But the Executive Council also needs to be free. It needs to have the freedom not to do something for which it cannot take responsibility. With some goodwill people will understand the need for such things. They can take what I am saying now and ask themselves whether they can commit to referring to the Executive Council for everything anthroposophical. If that is not the case the Executive Council has the right to refuse to recognize the matter in question as anthroposophical. That would mean it is not prepared to work with those who want to start their own anthroposophy somewhere. These are serious matters that need to be taken very seriously from now on.

There has also been a great deal of talk about the Society's publicity, especially the publication of the lecture cycles. This is a matter that cannot be taken seriously enough. We see evidence of this all the time. This morning Dr Unger showed me a new book by Hans Leisegang, entitled *The Occult Sciences,* which was published as part of Perthes' Educational Library series. Friedrich Andreas Perthes in Gotha/Stuttgart is one of the most renowned publishers.

You need to understand what Leisegang's denunciation means if it appears today in one of the most renowned publishing houses. It is important to understand how serious this is. Leisegang's little book contains a note which reads:

> A spiritual revolt against the so far unknown cycles by Rudolf Steiner! Hans Leisegang, *Die Geheimwissenschaften* [The occult sciences]. This book—an important new publication in Perthes' Educational Library—provides a broad overview of the state of research into occultism today, complete with numerous references for further study. The author strictly distinguishes between scientific occultism and the occult insights, presented as occult science, of spiritualists, theosophists and anthroposophists.

The words 'spiritual revolt against the so far unknown cycles by Rudolf Steiner' should induce us to make these cycles public at once—if they were not already public. We anticipated this because our opponents engage radically and vociferously with the most recent cycles. They are hardly printed when our opponents get hold of them and talk about them. They are discussed more eagerly by our opponents than by anthroposophists. Keeping the cycles secret would be absurd in the light of these developments; it would make us more vulnerable.

Much has been said since the Christmas Conference about the publication of the cycles. What is missing in all this is the earnestness that such a cause requires. I would like to say that the members of the First Class must be a Society of anthroposophical earnestness.

Much of what the Christmas Conference has achieved has not yet risen to full consciousness. It remains to be seen if we can now establish the First Class in practice. I therefore ask you again—so that we have a clear overview of the dear friends who wish to take part in the School here in Dornach—to write down your name on the sheets I will hand out, one sheet for every two rows, and to return them to my desk here. Please only write your name; all further information will be in your letters, I trust. If you did not mention in your letter of application how long you have been a member, please write it down now.

I shall let you know on Friday how we will go about giving out membership cards to those who have been admitted. We hope to make this process more pleasant than the collection of the application letters has been. That did not happen in one place, rather they were given to me here and there, wherever people met me, pressing them into my left or right hand in passing without considering how difficult it is for someone who is very busy to keep them in a particular order. I hope this can be done in a more orderly fashion.

[*Translated by Margot M. Saar*]

Newsletter, 10 February 1924

IV.

Those joining this School as a member are in a very different position from those joining the Anthroposophical Society. People become members of this School when they have been Society members for long enough. They have come to know what anthroposophy wants, what it really is. They have been able to form a judgement on what it can mean for them. The intention to join the School relies on the intention to take on certain duties and on the conscious wish to be a representative of the anthroposophical work.

Given the way anthroposophy is presented within the Anthroposophical Society, it is not only absurd, but also in bad taste when opponents falsely claim that anthroposophy seeks to indoctrinate. Those who engage with anthroposophy know this or at least they could know it. When members who left the Society claim that to be the case, they speak an objective untruth. In the Society no one is led to anthroposophy blindfolded. No one can therefore become a member of the School who is not fully awake to the tasks of anthroposophy.

People judge for themselves whether they wish to join the School once they have got to know the Anthroposophical Society as members. They will know exactly what is meant when the School's leadership speaks of members' duties. This also implies that the School's leadership cannot fulfil *its* tasks if members do not take on such duties. The relationship of each School member with the leadership remains one of complete freedom even though such duties are taken on, for the School leadership must also be free to act in accordance with its working conditions. It would not have this freedom were it unable to say to those who can choose freely whether or not to join the School: 'If I am to work with you, you must commit to meeting certain conditions.'

It shouldn't really be necessary to point all this out. But I need to say it because too often we hear statements like: 'If you join the School you have to give up some of your "human liberties".' If Society members say such things, it is hardly surprising when malevolent opponents accuse anthroposophy of turning its supporters into submissive tools of its evil intentions. Anyone who has taken part in the work of the Society for long enough will know that anthroposophy would become meaningless as soon as it went against the independent, prudent and insightful will of its members. Anthroposophy could not achieve its goals with submissive, spineless followers because it relies on the free will of its members.

[*Translated by Margot M. Saar*]

Newsletter, 17 February 1924

V.

Once they have accepted the conditions described, the members of the School will transform the Anthroposophical Society into something that alone can justify its existence. The starting point for the School's activities will have to be the Goetheanum. It is here where its tasks will first have to be accomplished. Ways and means will also be found to fully involve the School members who are scattered around the world. This cannot be achieved if everyone tries at once to get hold of transcripts of what was said at the Goetheanum. We experienced such a torrent about a year ago when word went around that the Society needed new life breathing into it.

Such rash behaviour is not helpful. On Friday 15 February I will give my first lecture for the School of Spiritual Science at the Goetheanum, initially for members who have been admitted to the School by the Executive Council. If you applied and have not had a response, you cannot consider yourself admitted. The School will gradually be fully established and all admissions will be processed.

As we continue our work in the School, it will also become apparent what needs to be done from the Goetheanum so that the work can grow. In this respect, ways and means also need to be found where the centre of the School is to be created. We will find ways of contacting the individuals and groups who let us know that they are seeking membership. However, people need to bear in mind that we will not manage here at the Goetheanum if existing institutions simply say: 'We are here and we want to join the Goetheanum and its School of Spiritual Science now!' Such declarations are of course good in themselves and the Executive Council at the Goetheanum will be delighted to receive them. But they cannot be put forward in the spirit of 'We are coming to you now, *this instant*; please make us members of the School at once.' All that would lead to is that everyone would continue doing what they were doing before whilst claiming they are doing it under the auspices of the School.

What is intended with the activities of the Executive Council at the Goetheanum can only gradually stream into the individual institutions. The Executive Council's task can only be to work, not to organize. In addition, it strives to bring the results of its work to those who want to have them. One can be ever so good at 'organizing' but that will do nothing for an institution like the Anthroposophical Society. It lives only from the *work* that is being done within it. The participation of the entire membership in the work at the Goetheanum would be the best way of ensuring the thriving of the Society. The Executive Council will do all it can to make everything that happens through the members the content of the Society.

[*Translated by Margot M. Saar*]

Newsletter, 24 February 1924

VI.

One more Section should be added to the ones about to be established by the Executive Council of the Anthroposophical Society. This can happen if the Executive Council's intentions meet with a positive response. Youth has stood in opposition to the older generation at all times; many a person has found comfort in this commonplace. Yet, *this kind of comfort* can easily lead to disaster.

Young people today—both their alarming aberrations and their more than justified search for something different from what the older generation offers them—should be understood out of the 'spirit of the times'. There are those young people whose life circumstances push them towards an academic career. They are presented with 'science'—solid, safe science that bears fruit in the external life. There is no point in complaining about this science in the way many non-scientists do. And yet, it leaves young souls feeling inwardly frozen before they have the chance to understand its solidity and safety, its fruitfulness for the outer life.

Science owes its greatness to the strong opposition it encountered from the mid-nineteenth century onwards. It became apparent then how easily people sail into the uncertainty of knowledge once they rise from the valleys of research to the heights of philosophy. People felt they had experienced repellent examples of such elevation. So they tried to liberate 'science' from philosophy. Science was to hold on to the 'facts' found in the valleys of nature and avoid the heights of the spirit. This opposition to philosophy evoked a certain inner satisfaction and the fighters against philosophy rejoiced in their antagonism.

Young people today can no longer share this joy. Their experience of the struggle against the 'uncertainty' and 'fantasy' of philosophy no longer fills their souls with satisfaction for there is nothing left to fight against. It is no longer possible to support the liberation of science from philosophy because philosophy is dead.

In contrast, youth has discovered something in its feeling life: no rational discovery but one that arises out of the whole, undivided human nature. It has discovered that no dignified human life is possible without philosophy. Many of the older generation heard the 'evidence' against philosophy and submitted to its power.

Young people no longer succumb to the rational power of this evidence. Instinctively they sense the powerlessness of rational evidence where the human heart speaks with unconquerable urgency. They experience science as solid but it owes it solidity to the absence of philosophy. Young people ask for philosophy. And yet, science needs young people.

At the Goetheanum we wish to support young people as they find ways to philosophy. And we hope that in the light of philosophy a true love for science can be kindled. We will not try to lose science in ideological dreams but to gain it more fully in conscious spirit-experience.

The Anthroposophical Society's Executive Council asks young people if they are willing to understand it, too. If this understanding can be found, the 'Section for the Spiritual Striving of Youth' will be able to carry strong forces into life.

[Further Newsletter contribution by Rudolf Steiner on the Youth Section and relevant events can be found in GA 260a. We include only one more report from the work of the School of Spiritual Science which followed on from a report about a pedagogical conference:]

[*Translated by Margot M. Saar*]

Newsletter, 20 April 1924

VII.

To the Members,
The lectures now being held for the general anthroposophical part of the School for Spiritual Science are intended to offer an overview of the experience of the 'threshold' between the sensory- and supersensory worlds. It is necessary for anyone who genuinely seeks knowledge of the human being to realize how everything 'nature' reveals in the way of beauty, greatness, the sublime, cannot lead to the human being. For the source of our inner being—the one who is creative in the outer world—is not in the natural world but in the spiritual world. However, neither the senses nor a brain-bound understanding can penetrate into this world—they must cease to be active if we seek to approach the world of their origin. At the point where this activity ceases, we are at first confronted with our inability to perceive anything at all. We survey our surroundings and darkness appears to us like a 'nothingness' that is there because of our inability to perceive. This inability will give way to capacities for spirit vision only if we become aware of higher powers in ourselves that create a 'sense of the spirit' just as the organism's physical forces create a sense of the body. A complete transformation of the inner human being from one form of existence into another is required. In the process of this transformation, we should not lose the one form of existence before we have achieved the other. A genuine transformation is the result of a genuine experience at the 'threshold'. Knowledge of the true human nature is possible only from a vantage point beyond the threshold. Anyone who wishes to use their healthy human understanding to take up reports about the far side of the threshold brought by someone with knowledge of that realm must also have an idea of what the one offering that knowledge experienced at the threshold. For only when we know the conditions under which this supersensible knowledge is acquired will we be in a position to judge it in the right way.

We will be able to provide content for the words that express the results of supersensible perception only if we understand what the individual who perceived it underwent before they had the power to coin such words. Without this understanding, the words appear to have a sense-bound rather than a supersensible meaning. As a result confusion sets in. The words become deceptive; instead of knowledge, illusion arises.

These indications are intended to offer a preliminary characterization for the esoteric activity of the School for Spiritual Science. Members who live at a distance will receive this content in an appropriate form as soon as the work required of us as a result of the Goetheanum Christmas Conference has progressed to the point that such a step is possible. What is said here exoterically will be developed in the School esoterically.

[*Translated by Marguerite Miller and Douglas Miller*]

Concerning the publication of the content of the First Class of the School of Spiritual Science

During the refounding of the Anthroposophical Society at Christmas 1923/1924 as the General Anthroposophical Society, Rudolf Steiner also reconstituted, as the School of Spiritual Science, the Esoteric School he had led in three classes from 1904 to 1914, at the same time extending its scope by adding artistic and scientific Sections. However, owing to the onset of his illness in the autumn of 1924 and his death on 30 March 1925 he was only able to make a beginning by establishing the First Class and the Sections. The actual step from the Esoteric School to the School of Spiritual Science was nevertheless an exceptional one. The Esoteric School from Helena Blavatsky's time had been secret. Its existence was known only to those personally invited to participate. In contrast, the existence of the School of Spiritual Science was stated openly in the public Statutes of the General Anthroposophical Society.

From the 1923 Christmas Conference onwards Rudolf Steiner worked within this publicly acknowledged framework. There are shorthand reports of 29 of the 38 Lessons of the class he was able to give before falling ill. These reports, minutely scrutinized in conjunction with all the relevant extant material, are published herewith as a means of securing their authenticity and their connection with the complete works of Rudolf Steiner because the general copyright on these works is due to expire at the end of 1995.

Rudolf Steiner did not wish in his time to have these texts released for personal reading. He did, however, agree that they should be recorded in shorthand, and he also arranged for the shorthand reports to be transcribed and typewritten. The strict rules of the School laid down that the content was to be passed on by word of mouth. Rudolf Steiner wished the rules to be understood not as arbitrary regulations, but as something belonging to the School's very nature. Some of his most important remarks concerning the establishment and the inner life of the First Class are therefore quoted here.

> With this lesson I wish to restore the School of Spiritual Science as an esoteric institution to the real task from which it has been threatening to become estranged during recent years. [Lesson One, Dornach, 15 February 1924]

> What is essential in this case [seeking admission to the School] is that those who become members of this School assume the responsibility—out of the spiritual essence, out of the occult spirit of this

School—with all their thinking, feeling and willing to be a worthy representative of anthroposophy before the world. Membership in this School is not possible in any other way. The decision whether or not someone is a worthy member of this School rests solely in the hands of the leadership of this School. The leadership of the School must take seriously the duties which it imposes on itself. The leadership of this School is responsible only to the spiritual powers, to the Michael power, for what it undertakes. The leadership must take seriously the point that members of this School must be worthy representatives of anthroposophy before the world. [First Recapitulation Lesson, Dornach, 6 September 1924]

Above all we must make ourselves responsible for feeling that we can seriously stand by every word we speak as being the absolute truth. Untrue statements, even when they emanate from what is termed good intentions, are something that acts destructively within an esoteric movement. We must be under no illusion as regards this fact; we must be absolutely clear about it. Intentions are not what matter, for people frequently take intentions quite lightly. Objective truth is what matters. It is one of the foremost duties of esoteric pupils to feel obliged not merely to say what they believe to be true, but to check whether what they are saying is indeed objectively true. Only if we serve by means of objective truth the divine, spiritual powers whose forces weave in this School shall we be able to steer our way through all the difficulties that will beset anthroposophy. [Lesson Seven, Dornach, 11 April 1924]

More than this: We should really avoid thinking of such a thing at all unless we can at the same time summon up the right inner mood for it. Above all, for such a thing as has been given in today's lesson, we ought to think of it only when we are really able to call forth within our soul this mood, which consists simply in this: that we first feel how the majesty comes to us, as with a voice of thunder, from worldwide cosmic spaces; then, in between, in a voice of gentle admonition, what comes from the Guardian of the Threshold; and finally, speaking deeply, penetratingly into our soul, what actually comes from one of the hierarchies.

Only on those occasions when we can remember this and can also summon up the feelings that are connected with the remembering of it, should we so much as think of these mantras or enter into them at all in our inner life. This is so that we do not desecrate them, even inwardly, or deprive them of their holiness and power by thinking of them with the ordinary dry and commonplace kind of thinking—with which we shall, after all, be thinking of them if we do not first put ourselves into the right mood of soul.

Because this is so, we should altogether bring about that mood of soul which feels that human self-knowledge is a holy thing, earnest and sublime. These things should only be uttered by the soul—even inwardly, let alone outwardly—in such a way that they are felt in all their earnestness, solemnity and holiness.

It is a great hindrance to progress on an esoteric path that these things are so often talked about in a cliquish kind of way—even with a touch of vanity; or as idle gossip, where the mood of earnestness and consecration is not at the same time aroused. When this happens, one is forgetting that in the esoteric life all depends on truth prevailing, on complete truth and sincerity prevailing. One can accomplish nothing whatsoever in esoteric life if one does not know that in esoteric life truth—absolute truth—must prevail, and that we cannot merely speak of truth and still persist in taking these things in the way one would in the profane, external life. Yet this is precisely what we do when we make these things the subject of commonplace and idle conversation. [Lesson Twelve, Dornach, 11 May 1924]

In Paragraph 7 of the Statutes of the General Anthroposophical Society instituted at Christmas 1923, Rudolf Steiner reserved for himself the task of designating a possible successor.[94] *However, he did not expressly do this. Since his death the endeavour has been to cultivate the content of the First Class in the manner he would have wished. However, it proved impossible to prevent the texts from spreading beyond those for whom they were originally intended. Responsibility for publishing the texts, should the necessity for this arise, would have rested with Mrs Marie Steiner, who inherited his estate in accordance with his will. Therefore, especially in the later years of her life, she struggled with the problem of how this might be done in a manner appropriate for the future. Some of her more important remarks concerning this are quoted below.*

How can we preserve the treasure with which we have been entrusted? Not by hiding it away, thereby simply giving our enemies the opportunity to do what they want with it, but by trusting in the good spiritual powers and giving new generations the possibility of receiving a stimulus in their souls that will kindle the spiritual light slumbering there, a light that will awaken in their souls what the powers of destiny have sown in them. [Letter of 4 January 1948]

At that time [in 1925, when the mantras carried by a prominent member of the First Class were confiscated during a journey to Russia], Mr Steffen[95] said something that has pursued me ever since. He said: 'I would make them [the texts of the class lessons] generally available.' I was very shocked at the time, heartily startled—yet, at the same time, I did wonder whether this might not be the best protection. [Letter of 4 January 1948]

I can only take on this work [reading the class lessons] if I can find that it fits into the context of all that I received by way of instructions, teachings, insights into his inmost thoughts, expressions of will, during the decades in which I collaborated with Dr Steiner ... He objected energetically to giving anyone the transcripts to read, even the most prominent bearers of the work in other countries who came to Dornach for a brief visit and wanted to read them in our house. He stated categorically that they did not exist. In endeavouring to understand what these words mean to me, I reach the following conclusion: it was not[96] his will that these lectures were only to be read aloud ... He said over and over again in connection with the esoteric lessons, and also, as we find recorded in the transcripts, in connection with the class lessons: These things must only be approached in the right mood of soul. [From notes on introductory words before reading a class lesson, in Notebook No. 20]

We have been guided towards the words 'Know Yourself' in inner freedom and in accordance with our own responsibility. We make a vow to our higher I with regard to the duty incumbent on us in respect of the School. The Leader of the School has been taken away from us on the physical plane. All the more strongly must we endeavour to be worthy of the spiritual guidance which he has not withdrawn from us, but for which, rather, he has given us strong guiding lines that are filled with his life and which can kindle the life in us if we unfold what he described as the necessary attitude of soul, the mood, in which we approach the spiritual words we receive ... A moral requirement is, then, the first thing we have to fulfil. It is the requirement of anthroposophy: wisdom lies solely in truth. We must transform wisdom and truth into deeds. To do this we have to work resolutely at forming our character. Rudolf Steiner stressed this requirement throughout the whole of his life's work, but he entrusted its fulfilment to our own free choice ... . [From Notebook No. 133]

> I now know full well that the wisdom contained in this work cannot be withheld from humankind. But nothing must be too much for us when we endeavour to weigh up how to administer it in the right way. I therefore include in my considerations another factor: the guideline he himself gave to a group whose members wished to experience the mantras together. The person who spoke the mantras was to work out for him or herself what to say that could bring about a connection with the mantras. In other words, he wanted people to do their own independent work with regard to the verses, though based, of course, on the wisdom that had been imparted to them. But most important of all was the actual experience of the verses. [From Notebook No. 20]

The above quotations are given to stress the essential commitments laid by Rudolf Steiner on those who wanted to receive the wisdom of the First Class: serious inward work, and great responsibility, in order to become 'a worthy representative of the anthroposophical cause before the whole world with all one's thinking, feeling and willing'.

Having become acquainted with these thoughts we soon and repeatedly find ourselves asking with concern whether it might not be altogether wrong to publish these texts at all. In the passages cited above as well as in many other places Rudolf Steiner explained with great urgency that this School can only develop its potential under the discipline of strict inner cohesion and that it will lose its power if the content finds its way to people who are not authorized members of the School. In the light of such statements how can publication be justified?

The instructions quoted above were intended to form a basis for an enclosed circle held together in strictest discipline, and such a circle did indeed exist in Rudolf Steiner's time. After his death, however, its privacy was soon breached. Mantras and texts found their way into entirely unauthorized hands. In addition, as time has gone on, the mantras have been copied from blackboards thousands of times. Such handwritten copies were intended for personal study but after the death of the owners very many of them were not returned to the School. Today they are scattered across the world in an entirely uncontrollable fashion.

The present publication of these texts within the framework of the complete works of Rudolf Steiner is being undertaken in answer to this situation. In addition, the general copyright protection of his work is about to run out, and it is very important that everything stemming from him should remain linked with his name and with the context of his work as a whole in the eyes of the world. The work must not be left open to any possibility of obscure publishing ventures.

The present publication of this work thus poses serious questions of which only some aspects can be touched on here. Two more points may be mentioned briefly: even though the texts now published contain clear statements that strenuous measures should be undertaken to protect them from publication, nevertheless it should not be forgotten that these very measures were originated by Rudolf Steiner whose chief deed has been to publish in an unprecedented manner knowledge previously kept secret. Perhaps this view of the matter can lead to an understanding that at a later point in time things might become accessible which before could not possibly be public. Even though as a consequence of Rudolf Steiner's death it seems impossible to continue putting into practice the intentions on which the First Class was based, it would not be right to think that the significance of the whole is now null and void as a result of the failure of certain individuals in this School and as a result of the pressure from outside to which the texts have been subjected. That this is not the case is borne out by experiences gained in many serious efforts to continue the work with the content of the School. These experiences have been possible despite the fact that the original conditions were no longer being fulfilled in all their initial strictness.

The present publication is being undertaken with this in mind. We can be guided today by what Rudolf Steiner said when he gave permission for the publication of his lectures which had initially been printed only for members of the Anthroposophical Society: 'This spirit of the age cannot tolerate the outer secret, but it can quite well tolerate the inner secret.' (Dornach, 28 December 1923, see The Christmas Conference for the Foundation of the General Anthroposophical Society, 1923/1924, p.152.) These words express the fact that although the 'outer secret' has fallen by the wayside, the 'inner secret' has become all the more important.

The work of the School of Spiritual Science has been carried on ever since Rudolf Steiner's death despite the existence of many diverging concepts of what this School actually is. Those who have been carrying on the work will have to understand that the situation described above means that this work in the First Class of the School of Spiritual Science and in the various Sections is attaining a new character. Increased significance now attaches to the condition laid down by Rudolf Steiner from the beginning for acceptance into the First Class which states that every member must be willing to be a worthy representative of the anthroposophical cause before the world, both as an individual student and together with all the other students of the School. In today's battle of the spirit with the most tremendous materialism on the one hand and with an almost inconceivable abundance of extremely questionable occult streams on the other all members must work together even more consciously in order to bring anthroposophy to proper effectiveness. In the future the conscious will to share in bearing this burden will increasingly have to be required as a condition of membership in the First Class of the School of Spiritual Science.

The texts are published, but the spiritual facts to which the mantras lead us remain 'inner secrets'. As ever, it remains the task of members of the First Class and of the Sections of the School of Spiritual Science to find paths to these true spiritual facts and experiences, as well as to make them fruitful for the culture of today.

Dornach, Spring 1992
For the Rudolf Steiner Nachlassverwaltung:
Edwin Froböse
Hella Wiesberger
Dr Gian-Andrea Balaster
For the School of Spiritual Science:
Manfred Schmidt-Brabant
Dr Hagen Bisanz
Jörgen Smit
(Translated by Marguerite and Douglas Miller)

From: Rudolf Steiner, *Esoterische Unterweisungen für die erste Klasse der Freien Hochschule für Geisteswissenschaft am Goetheanum*, Erster Band, GA 270/1, Dornach 1992, p. IX ff. [Title of English translation: *Esoteric Lessons for the First Class of the School of Spiritual Science at the Goetheanum*.]

Notes

1 Cf. Steiner, Rudolf: *How to Know Higher Worlds*, (GA 10), Hudson NY 1994, translator C. Bamford, p. 28.

2 See Appendix, lecture of 30 January 1924.

3 Steiner, Rudolf: *Autobiography*, Chapter 27, Great Barrington 2005, translator Rita Stebbing, p. 91.

4 Cf. Wiesberger, Hella: *Rudolf Steiner's Esoteric Teaching Activity,* Hudson NY 2019, translators R. Stebbing, J. Wood, M. Barton, M. Post.

5 Selg, Peter: *Die Intentionen Ita Wegmans 1925–1943* [Ita Wegman's intentions], Arlesheim 2019, p. 189ff.

6 For more information on this cf. Kiersch, Johannes: *A History of the School of Spiritual Science. The First Class.* Forest Row 2006, translator Anna R. Meuss. (An extended version of this book was published in German under the title: *Steiners individualisierte Esoterik einst und jetzt. Zur Entwicklung der Freien Hochschule für Geisteswissenschaft* [Steiner's individualized esotericism then and now. A history of the School of Spiritual Science], Dornach 2012.)

7 Cf. Steiner, Rudolf at the end of Lesson 19 of 2 August 1924, *Esoteric Lessons for the First Class of the School of Spiritual Science*, Forest Row 2020, various translators, volume 2, p. 335.

8 Steiner, Rudolf: *Karmic Relationships. Esoteric Studies, vols. 6 and 8.* Forest Row 2015, translator D.S. Osmond.

9 Ibid., lecture of 20 July 1924.

10 Letter from Helga Geelmuyden to Marie Steiner of 30 September 1947, cited in Johannes Kiersch: *Steiners individualisierte Esoterik einst und jetzt* [Steiner's individualized esotericism then and now], Dornach 2012, p. 134.

11 Zimmermann, Heinz: *Speaking, Listening, Understanding: The Art of Creating Conscious Conversation*, Stuttgart 1997, translator James Hindes.

12 Cf. Steiner, Rudolf: *How to Know Higher Worlds*, (GA 10), Hudson NY 1994, translator C. Bamford, Chapter 10 'The Guardian of the Threshold', p. 184-194; Steiner, Rudolf: *An Outline of Esoteric Science,* (GA 13), Chapter 'Knowledge of Higher Worlds', Hudson N.Y. 1997, translator C.E. Creeger; Steiner, Rudolf: *A Way to Self-Knowledge and the Threshold of the Spiritual World*, (GA 16/17), Great Barrington 1999, translator C. Bamford, Meditation 4, p. 26.

13 Steiner, Rudolf: *An Outline of Esoteric Science,* GA 13, Hudson NY 1997, translator Catherine E. Creeger. Cf. Steiner, Rudolf: *The Spiritual Hierarchies and the Physical World: Zodiac, Planets and Cosmos,* GA 110, Hudson NY 2008, translator René Querido; and Steiner, Rudolf: *Inner Experiences of Evolution,* GA 132, Great Barrington 2009, translator Jann Gates.

14 Steiner, Rudolf: *Die Konstitution der Allgemeinen Anthroposophischen Gesellschaft und der Freien Hochschule für Geisteswissenschaft. Der Wiederaufbau des Goetheanum 1924/25* [The Constitution of the General Anthroposophical Society and the School of Spiritual Science. Rebuilding the Goetheanum 1924/1925], GA 260a, p. 131f.

15 Ibid., p. 131.

16 Steiner, Rudolf: *Theosophy* (chapter: Destiny and the Reincarnation of the Spirit, GA 9, Hudson NY 1994, p. 89, translator Catherine E. Creeger.

17 Steiner, Rudolf: *Die Verbindung zwischen Lebenden und Toten* (GA 168, 3 December 1916), p. 214. (Steiner, Rudolf: *The Connection Between the Living and the Dead*, GA 168, Hudson NY 2017, translator Aria Jackson.)

18 Steiner, Rudolf: *Youth and the Etheric Heart*, GA 217a, Great Barrington 2007, p. 89, translator Catherine E. Creeger.

19 Ibid., p. 92.

20 Cf. Boutinet, Jean-Pierre: *Antropologia do projecto*, Lisboa 1990.

21 Steiner, Rudolf: *Youth and the Etheric Heart*, GA 217a, Great Barrington 2007, p. 92f., tr. Catherine E. Creeger.

22 Ibid., p. 92.

23 Steiner, Rudolf: *Anthroposophical Leading Thoughts*, GA 26 (first Leading Thought), Forest Row 1998, translator Mary Adams.

24 Steiner, Rudolf: *Understanding Healing: Meditative Reflections on Deepening Medicine through Spiritual Science,* GA 316, Forest Row 2013, translator Christian von Arnim.

25 Steiner, Rudolf: *Mantric Sayings. Meditations 1903–1925, Soul Exercises, 1903–1925.* GA 268, Great Barrington 2015, translator D. Fleming. Selg, Peter: *The Warmth Meditation. A Path to the Good in the Service of Healing*, Great Barrington 2016, translator Rory Bradley.

26 Steiner, Rudolf: *Rosicrucianism and Modern Initiation: Mystery Centres of the Middle Ages,* GA 233a, 13 January1924, Forest Row 2020, translators Mary Adams, Frederick Amrine.

27 Steiner, Rudolf: *Anthroposophy in the Light of Goethe's Faust,* GA 272 (22 May 1915), Great Barrington 2014, translator Frederick Amrine.

28 Cf. chapter 'The Guardian of the Threshold. Some Characteristics of Suprasensory Consciousness' in Steiner, Rudolf: *A Way of Self-Knowledge and the Threshold of the Spiritual World,* GA 16/17, Great Barrington 2006, translator Christopher Bamford.

29 Questions and Answers, 11 March 1920, in Steiner, Rudolf: *The Fourth Dimension. Sacred Geometry, Alchemy, and Mathematics*, GA324a, Great Barrington 2000, translator Catherine E. Creeger.

30 Gschwind, Peter: *Die Ich-Struktur der Materie* [The I-structure of matter], Verlag am Goetheanum, Dornach 2008.

31 Steiner, Rudolf: *Geisteswissenschaftliche Grundlagen zum Gedeihen der Landwirtschaft*, GA 327, Dornach 1979, p. 12. (Title of English translation: *Agriculture Course: The Birth of the Biodynamic Method*, Forest Row 2004, translator George Adams.)

32 Steiner, Rudolf: *Good and Evil Spirits and Their Influence on Humanity*, GA102, lecture of 1 June 1908, Forest Row 2014, translator Anna Meuss, p. 151.

33 See note 31, p. 27.

34 Ibid.

35 Ibid., p. 189.

36 Steiner, Rudolf: *The Michael Mystery*, GA 26, Hudson NY 1984, translator Marjorie Spock.

37 Steiner, Rudolf: *Eurythmie als sichtbare Sprache,* GA 279 (11 July 1924), Dornach 2019, p. 283. (Title of English translation: *Eurythmy as Visible Speech*, Forest Row 2019, translator A. Stott, M. Stott, C. Schmandt.)

38 In eurythmy for instance, cf. Steiner, Rudolf: *Eurythmy as Visible Speech,* lecture of 11 July 1924. See note 37.

39 Steiner, Rudolf: Das Tonerlebnis im Menschen, in: Steiner, Rudolf: *Eurythmie als sichtbarer Gesang,* GA 278 (8 March1923), Dornach 2015, p. 33. An English translation of the lecture of 8 March 1923 can be found in Steiner, Rudolf: *The Inner Nature of Music and the Experience of Tone*, GA 283, Hudson NY 1983, translator Maria St. Goar.

40 Cf. Steiner, Rudolf: *Okkulte Untersuchungen über das Leben zwischen Tod und neuer Geburt* [Occult investigations into life between death and a new birth], GA 140 (11 October 1913), Dornach 2003, pp. 349–350.

41 Rudolf Steiner to Lory Smits, the first eurythmist: 'This new art of movement can only be carried out by someone who recognizes and is convinced that human beings consist of body, soul and spirit.' in: Steiner, Rudolf: *Die Entstehung und Entwickelung der Eurythmie,* GA 277a (16 September 1912), Dornach 1982, p. 19. (Title of English translation: *Eurythmy, its Birth and Development.* Forest Row 2019, translator Alan Stott.)

42 Early drawing by Rudolf Steiner 'Relationship to the whole world/ relationship with one another/ relationship with the earth, gentle inner turning' in Steiner, Rudolf: *Die Entstehung und Entwickelung der Eurythmie,* GA 277a, (entry from 1912), p. 168. See note 41.

43 Steiner, Rudolf: *Vorträge über christlich-religiöses Wirken,* vol. II, (GA 343), Dornach 1993, p. 39. (Title of English translation: *The Foundation Course: Spiritual Discernment, Religious Feeling, Sacramental Action,* Fremont, Michigan 2022, translator Hanna von Maltitz.)

44 Steiner, Rudolf: 1918 notebook entry in *Wahrspruchworte*, GA 40, Dornach 1998, p. 217.

45 Steiner, Rudolf: *Aus den Inhalten der Esoterischen Schule, Bd. II, Esoterische Stunde vom 10. Oktober* 1911, GA 266/2, Dornach 1996, p. 215. (Title of

English translation: *From the Esoteric School, Esoteric Lessons 1910-1912*, Hudson NY 2012, Lesson of 10 October 1911, translator James H. Hindes.)

46 Steiner, Rudolf: *Der Zusammenhang des Menschen mit der elementarischen Welt*, GA 158, Dornach 1993, p. 127. (Title of English translation: *Our Connection with the Elemental World*, Forest Row 2016, translator Simon Blaxland-de Lange.)

47 Steiner, Rudolf: *Art as Seen in the Light of Mystery Wisdom*, GA 275 (4 February 1915), Forest Row 2010, p. 161, translators Pauline Wehrle, Johanna Collis.

48 Steiner, Rudolf: *Das Künstlerische in seiner Weltmission*, GA 276 (3 June1923), Dornach 2002, p. 62. (Title of English translation: *The Arts and Their Mission*, Lecture of 3 June 1923, Hudson NY 1986, translators Lisa D. Monges, V. Moore.)

49 See Caroline von Heydebrand's and Herbert Hahn's transcripts in Steiner, Rudolf: *The First Teachers Course, Anthropological Foundations, Methods of Teaching, Practical Discussions*, GA 293–295, Bangkok 2020, translator Margot M. Saar, p. 18f.

50 Steiner, Rudolf: *Balance in Teaching*, GA 302a (22 September 1920), Great Barrington 2007, translator René Querido, p. 44.

51 Steiner, Rudolf: *Towards Social Renewal*, GA 23, Forest Row 2000, translator Matthew Barton.

52 Cf. Steiner, Rudolf: *Spiritual Science and the Social Question*, an Essay, Dornach 1905/1906, Whitefish MT 2010, translator E. Bowen-Wedgwood.

53 Cf. Steiner, Rudolf: *Die soziale Grundforderung unserer Zeit. In geänderter Zeitlage, zwölf Vorträge, Dornach 1918 und Bern 1918*, GA186, Dornach 1990. (Some lectures in this book have been translated into English and can be found in: *The Challenge of the Times*, Hudson NY 1979, translator Olin D. Wannamaker.) Cf. Steiner, Rudolf: *Die soziale Zukunft* [Social future], 6 Lectures, Zurich 1919, GA 332a, Dornach 2019.
Cf. Steiner, Rudolf: *Rethinking Economics, 14 Lectures, Dornach 1922,* GA 340, Great Barrington 2013, translator Peter Clemm.
Steiner, Rudolf: *The Spiritual Ground of Education, 12 lectures, Oxford 1922,* GA 305, Great Barrington 2004, translator unknown.

54 Steiner, Rudolf: *Die soziale Grundforderung unserer Zeit. In geänderter Zeitlage. Zwölf Vorträge,* GA 187, Dornach 1990, p. 175. (Some lectures in this book have been translated into English and can be found in: *The Challenge of the Times*, Hudson NY 1979, translator Olin D. Wannamaker.)

55 Steiner, Rudolf: *The Philosophy of Freedom*, GA 4, Forest Row 2011. Translator Michael Wilson.

56 Steiner, Rudolf: *Gesammelte Aufsätze zur Kultur- und Zeitgeschichte 1887-1901* [Collected essays on cultural and contemporary history], GA 31, Dornach 1989.

57 Steiner, Rudolf: *Geisteswissenschaft und Soziale Frage* [Spiritual science and the social question], GA 34, Dornach 1989.

58 Steiner, Rudolf: *Sprüche, Dichtungen, Mantren* [Verses, poetry, mantras], GA 40a, Dornach 2002.

59 Barkhoff, Wilhelm Ernst: https://www.gls.de/privatkunden/gls-bank/aktuelles/presse/blumen-statt-fukushima-gls-bank-startet-zukunftsprojekte/

60 Cf. Chapter IV.

61 Steiner, Rudolf: *Anthroposophische Gemeinschaftsbildung,* GA 257, Dornach 1989, p. 60. (Title of English translation: *Awakening to Community*, Spring Valley 1974, translator Marjorie Spock.)

62 Steiner, Rudolf: *Four Mystery Dramas,* GA 14, Hudson NY 2007, tr. Ruth and Hans Pusch.

63 The association was named after the main protagonist in the Mystery Dramas, Johannes Thomasius.

64 Steiner, Rudolf: *Zur Geschichte des Johannesbau-Vereins und des Goetheanum-Vereins 1911–1924* [The history of the Johannes Building Association and the Goetheanum Association 1911–1924], GA 252, Dornach 2019, p. 17.

65 Cf. Steiner, Rudolf: *From the History and Contents of the First Section of the Esoteric School 1904-1914*, GA 264, Hudson NY 2010, translator John M. Wood; and Steiner, Rudolf: *Freemasonry and Ritual Work.* GA 265, Hudson NY 2007, translator John Wood.

66 Cf. Wiesberger, Hella: *Rudolf Steiner's Esoteric Teaching Activity. Truthfulness, Continuity, New Form*, Hudson NY 2019, translators Rita Stebbing, John Wood, Matthew Barton, Marsha Post.

67 Steiner, Rudolf: *Esoteric Lessons. From the Esoteric School,* GA 266 1–3, Great Barrington 2007–2012, translator James Hindes, Marsha Post.

68 See note 66.

69 Steiner, Rudolf: *From the History and Contents of the First Section of the Esoteric School 1904–1914*, GA 264, Hudson NY 2010, translator John M. Wood.

70 Steiner, Rudolf: *Lucifer Gnosis* 1902–1908, GA 34, Dornach 1987.

71 Steiner, Rudolf: *How to Know Higher Worlds*, GA 10, Hudson NY 1994, translator Christopher Bamford.

72 Rudolf Steiner was the first to make knowledge public that had been kept secret before, in particular the methodical foundations of such knowledge. Cf. the essay '*Frühere Geheimhaltung und jetzige Veröffentlichung übersinnlicher Erkenntnisse*' [Previous concealment and present publication of suprasensory insights] in Steiner, Rudolf: *Philosophie und Anthroposophie*, GA 35, Dornach 1984, p. 391f.

73 The Esoteric Lessons have been published as part of Rudolf Steiner's complete works, cf. Steiner, Rudolf: *Esoteric Lessons for the First Class of the School of*

Spiritual Science at the Goetheanum, bilingual edition, 2 volumes, Dornach/Forest Row 2020, various translators.

74 'The Essence and Task of Freemasonry from the Point of View of Spiritual Science', in Steiner, Rudolf: *The Temple Legend. Freemasonry and related occult movements,* GA 93, Forest Row 2014, translator John M. Wood, p. 69f.

75 The law of continuity demands that, in an existing esoteric context, one builds on existing forms, striving to develop them further and transform them. (Cf. Wiesberger, Hella: *Rudolf Steiner's Esoteric Teaching Activity,* see note 66.

76 Steiner, Rudolf: *Freemasonry and Ritual Work,* GA 265, Hudson NY 2007, translator John Wood.

77 Steiner, Rudolf: *Zur Geschichte des Johannesbau-Vereins und des Goetheanum-Vereins 1911–1924* [The history of the Johannes Building Association and the Goetheanum Association 1911–1924], GA 252, Dornach 2019, p.72f.

78 Ibid., p. 77.

79 Cf. Haid, Christiane: *Auf der Suche nach dem Menschen. Die anthroposophische Jugend- und Studentenarbeit in den Jahren 1920–31* [In search of the human being. Anthroposophical youth and student work 1920–1931], Dornach 2001.

80 Steiner, Rudolf: *Das Schicksalsjahr 1923 in der Geschichte der Anthroposophischen Gesellschaft. Vom Goetheanumbrand zur Weihnachtstagung* [1923–the fateful year in the history of the Anthroposophical Society. From the fire at the Goetheanum to the Christmas Conference], GA 259, Dornach 1991.

81 Rudolf Steiner referred to the Celestial Hierarchy of Dionysius the Areopagite.

82 See note 68. GA 266/1, lessons of 18 and 23 October 1907 in Berlin.

83 Steiner, Rudolf: *Approaching the Mystery of Golgotha,* GA 152, Hudson NY 2006, translator Michael Miller.

84 According to Rudolf Steiner's spiritual-historical research seven different archangels alternately reign as formative spirits of time, changing every 300 years.

85 For more detail see Steiner, Rudolf: *The Philosophy of Freedom*, GA 4, Forest Row 2011, translator Michael Wilson.

86 Steiner, Rudolf: *The Christmas Conference for the Foundation of the General Anthroposophical Society 1923/1924*, GA 260, Hudson NY 1990, translators Johanna Collis, Michael Wilson.

87 Steiner, Rudolf: *World History and the Mysteries in the Light of Anthroposophy,* GA 233, Forest Row 2021, various translators.

88 Steiner, Rudolf: *Die Weihnachtstagung zur Begründung der Allgemeinen Anthroposophischen Gesellschaft 1923/24*, GA 260, Dornach 1994, p. 60ff. (For details of English translation of this book see note 87.)

89 Steiner, Rudolf: *Die Konstitution der Allgemeinen Anthroposophischen Gesellschaft und der Freien Hochschule für Geisteswissenschaft. Der Wiederaufbau des Goetheanum 1924/25* [The Constitution of the General Anthroposophical Society and the School of Spiritual Science. Rebuilding the Goetheanum 1924/1925], GA 260a.

90 Steiner, Rudolf: *Karmic Relationships. Esoteric Studies, volumes 1 to 8,* volumes 6 and 8 in particular, Forest Row 2015, translator D.S. Osmond.

91 Steiner, Rudolf: *Anthroposophical Leading Thoughts. Anthroposophy as a Path of Knowledge: the Michael Mystery*, GA 26, Forest Row 2007, translators George and Mary Adams.

92 Steiner, Rudolf: *Karmic Relationships. Esoteric Studies* (GA 235–240), Forest Row 2015, translator D.S. Osmond.

93 Steiner, Rudolf: *Anthroposophical Leading Thoughts* (see note 92 for details), and Steiner, Rudolf: *Karmic Relationships. Esoteric Studies* (see note 91 for details).

94 'The organizing of the School of Spiritual Science is, to begin with, the responsibility of Rudolf Steiner, who will appoint his collaborators and his possible successor.'

95 Albert Steffen (1884–1963). After Rudolf Steiner's death the first president of the General Anthroposophical Society.

96 The word *not* is missing in the 1992 edition of GA270/71and also in the 1994 English edition (*Esoteric Lessons of the First Class of the School of Spiritual Science at the Goetheanum*).

A note from the publisher

For more than a quarter of a century, **Temple Lodge Publishing** has made available new thought, ideas and research in the field of spiritual science.

Anthroposophy, as founded by Rudolf Steiner (1861-1925), is commonly known today through its practical applications, principally in education (Steiner-Waldorf schools) and agriculture (biodynamic food and wine). But behind this outer activity stands the core discipline of spiritual science, which continues to be developed and updated. True science can never be static and anthroposophy is living knowledge.

Our list features some of the best contemporary spiritual-scientific work available today, as well as introductory titles. So, visit us online at **www.templelodge.com** and join our emailing list for news on new titles.

If you feel like supporting our work, you can do so by buying our books or making a direct donation (we are a non-profit/ charitable organisation).

office@templelodge.com

TEMPLE LODGE

For the finest books of Science and Spirit